A Practical Guide to
Tiering Instruction in the Differentiated Classroom

Sarah Armstrong With Stephanie Haskins

Classroom-Tested Strategies, Management Tools,
Assessment Ideas, and More to Help You Create
Effective Tiered Lessons That Work for Every Learner

SCHOLASTIC

New York • Toronto • London • Auckland • Sydney
Mexico City • New Delhi • Hong Kong • Buenos Aires

Acknowledgements

I would like to give thanks to

Stephanie Haskins, a teacher of teachers, who understands what it is to practice differentiation with diverse students and effectively communicates these understandings to colleagues;

My editor, Joanna Davis-Swing who was a consistent advocate and critical friend throughout the process;

My family and friends who believe it is not if, but when.

Cover design by Jorge J. Namerow
Interior design by Sarah Morrow

Copyright © 2010 by Sarah Armstrong
All rights reserved. Published by Scholastic Inc.
Printed in the U.S.A.
ISBN-13: 978-0-545-11266-6
ISBN-10: 0-545-11266-4

5 6 7 8 9 10   40   17 16 15 14 13

Contents

Foreword 5

Chapter 1 ✐ **Differentiation in Practice: Tiered Instruction** 6

Differentiation at a Glance 6
Step by Step: Moving Toward Differentiation 7
Why Tiered Instruction? 8
Ready to Begin 12
Ideas for Reflection 12

Chapter 2 ✐ **Knowing Your Learners: Assessing and Scaffolding to Meet Students' Needs** 14

Assessing Reading Levels 15
The Role of Assessment in the Differentiated Classroom 16
Assessment *for* Learning 17
A Range of Assessments 21
Self-Assessment of Learning 22
Tracking Results 24
Ongoing Assessment 25
Scaffolding: The Link Between Assessment and Instruction 25
Assessing by Tuning in to What Students Know and What They Don't 26
The Management of Scaffolding 27
Taking the Next Step 32
Feedback as Part of the Assessment Picture 33
Summary 34
Ideas for Reflection 34

Chapter 3 ✐ **Lesson Design With Tiering in Mind** 35

Activating Prior Knowledge: Strategies for Reeling in Learners 37
Providing a Powerful APK Experience 38
Using APK: Discussion and Data to Assess Students' Background Knowledge .. 42
APK and the Curriculum 45
Chunking the Lesson 46
Keeping Students Engaged: Movement Keeps Learners on Track 47
A Lesson Planning Template 50
Summary 50
Ideas for Reflection 50

Chapter 4 ✐ **Content Instruction: Tiering to Teach Essential Skills and Knowledge** 51

Knowing the *What* of the Lesson 52
A Tiered Instruction Imperative: Choosing Content Based on Instructional Reading Levels 53

Using Supplemental Nonfiction Books to Tier Content Instruction 57

Expanding Beyond the Textbook... 57

Rewriting to Adapt Texts 62

Tiering Vocabulary 64

Summary.. 65

Ideas for Reflection 66

Chapter 5 ☙ Process: Strategic Teaching to Tier Instruction .. 67

Tiering a Lesson: Common Goals Using Different Strategies................. 71

Entry Points 72

Complex Thinking Is for *All* Students.. 79

Differentiating With Divergent Questions 82

Managing the Process of Tiering 83

Strategies for Assigning and Managing Tiered Tasks 84

Tiering With Personal Agendas 87

Selecting Graphic Organizers for Tiered Instruction 91

Adjusting Social Interaction 93

Summary.. 97

Ideas for Reflection 98

Chapter 6 ☙ Product: Tiering Ways Students Demonstrate What They Know 99

Expanding Perspectives About Assessment 100

Authentic Assessments 104

Adapting Assessments to Students' Strengths................................ 106

Providing "Look Fors" for Students 107

Students as Partners in Assessment.. 108

Creating Self-Assessments 109

Rubrics 109

Coaching Students With Self-Assessments 113

Incorporating Student Choice Into Assessment Design 114

Tips for Developing Assessments... 116

Tiering: Providing Support and Extension 118

Grading Tiered Products 119

Summary.. 122

Ideas for Reflection 123

Chapter 7 ☙ Tiered Instruction: How to Get There From Here .. 124

Growing as Differentiators.. 124

The Power of Collaboration.. 126

Team Versus Group... 127

Students as Partners 130

Summary 130

Ideas for Reflection 131

Bibliography 132

Appendix 138

Foreword

An educator attending a conference where I presented a couple of summers ago said to me with some exasperation, "Do you see differentiation connected to everything in the classroom?" I thought the question was interesting because I'd never considered it before, so I paused for a second before I gave her the answer she didn't want to hear. "That's a great question, and yes, I think I do see differentiation connected with pretty much everything in the classroom," I said. I went on to explain my thinking a bit, but I don't think I helped her quandary.

The educator's discomfort, I believe, was that she wanted someone to make differentiation simple. She was in search of "differentiation lite." That's understandable, of course. It's not helpful to feel overwhelmed. We all need a place to start a long journey, but we also need to understand the nature of the journey on which we might become a traveler. To grow as educators, we need both a rich topographic map of the terrain before us and clear directions and guideposts for each leg of the journey.

This book is the rare find on the topic of differentiation that both connects differentiation with multiple elements in a classroom system and provides detailed guidance necessary to grow in proficiency with tiering and as a teacher. Sarah Armstrong shows readers the scope and power of tiering when it is used appropriately. In the process, she, with numerous contributions of examples, illustrations, and assessments from Stephanie Haskins, reminds us that effective tiering must adhere to the principles of "defensible differentiation," including her insistence that tiering should be used to "teach up" to the full range of learners, not to "water down" content for students who may struggle to learn. She shows readers how to incorporate standards into tiered lessons—and also how to ensure that tiering is a catalyst for complex thinking for all learners. She makes clear how tiering intersects with content, process, and product. She reminds us how it is that curriculum, assessment, and instruction are inextricably interwoven in a strong classroom. She models how effective record keeping, feedback, and collaboration benefit both teacher and students. She demonstrates how rubrics and other indicators of quality work support students in extending their reach. She simply understands that there is no such thing as quality differentiation except in the context of quality instruction as a whole.

This book is a serious tool for teachers who take their craft seriously. Those teachers will read the book again and again, mark it up, draw from it, and return each time more competent and confident in addressing students' readiness differences—and in what it means to teach well!

Carol Tomlinson
University of Virginia

Chapter 1

Differentiation in Practice: Tiered Instruction

The phrase "one size fits all" most certainly does *not* apply to instruction in today's diverse classrooms. Each school day a dynamic mix of learners walk into classrooms, students who differ by performance levels, learning styles, gender, ethnicity, race, and socioeconomics. If we take into account variables such as health, disabilities, stressful life incidents, and level of family support for education, the picture becomes even more complex. Yet each of these unique children needs to be educated as a citizen of and contributor to the twenty-first-century world. And it is our job to teach all of them.

Differentiation at a Glance

Differentiated instruction counters the traditional mind-set that all students can be taught at the same pace, from the same materials, using the same teaching strategies, in the same groups, day after day.

Differentiation entails planning instruction that recognizes students have different entry points for learning new content, unique background experiences that help facilitate learning, and specific interests and learning styles that—when tapped into—can elevate achievement. Teachers who differentiate pre-assess to find out what their students already know and use this information to guide instruction and grouping. Though many aspects of differentiation will be discussed in this book, what's of greatest importance is that teachers recognize the *need* to differentiate and that they have the heart to do so. The tools and techniques can be acquired.

Even committed, well-intentioned teachers struggle with differentiating instruction. One common challenge is acquiring the repertoire of teaching strategies and resources that will help teachers implement differentiation.

Though the clock can't be stopped, I hope to provide a wide range of tools and ideas that will give you increased confidence and greater facility in planning for your diverse learners. As you implement these ideas, differentiation will become an integral part of your teaching. You will soon acquire a rhythm or establish a system that facilitates the process.

Step by Step: Moving Toward Differentiation

My intention in writing this book is to help you acquire a secure footing as you seek a balance between meeting the demands of the curriculum and differentiating instruction for your students. I have narrowed our topic somewhat, focusing on differentiating through tiered instruction. Carol Ann Tomlinson, a leader in the field of differentiation, defines *tiering* as "a readiness-based instructional approach in which all students work with the same essential knowledge, understanding, and skill, but at different levels of difficulty based on their current proficiency with the ideas and skills" (2006, p. 107). Successful tiered instruction allows a student to work with the essential content at an appropriate level of challenge. For this to happen, teachers must design lessons and choose activities that are easily adapted to various skill levels.

Many of us are working in schools that have a Response to Intervention (RtI) commitment. The language of RtI frequently refers to tiers 1, 2, and 3, with first-tier services occurring in the general education classroom and the second- and third-tier services provided by tutors and intervention specialists in small-group or individualized settings (Fuchs & Fuchs, 2005). The National Center on Response to Intervention refers to the first level of intervention as the *primary* level where students are taught the core academic curriculum in the classroom, with some adaptations made by the classroom teacher. The *secondary* level of intervention refers to students who are not responsive to the primary level and will benefit from small-group tutoring, most often provided by trained tutors. The *tertiary* level focuses on intense, individualized interventions for students with longer and more frequent sessions (2008). Although differentiating instruction is a key component of any RtI framework, the RtI tiers are distinct from the "tiers" in tiered instruction, which is the focus of this book. To distinguish between RtI tiers and the clustering or grouping of students for tiered instruction, I will simply refer to groups formed for a particular tiered lesson or activity by number: Group 1, Group 2, and so on.

The decision to differentiate often begins with an examination of one's personal belief system. *Do I recognize the diversity of achievement, interests, and needs in my classroom? Am I committed to designing instruction that addresses these differences?* If the answer to both these questions is yes, then differentiation is a goal to pursue, and this book will provide support, direction, templates, and models to fulfill that commitment.

Why Tiered Instruction?

When you tier instruction, you acknowledge that the content is appropriate for all students. You also acknowledge that to reach your learners, both the content and the methods of teaching must be adapted. Tiered instruction is not the only component of differentiation, but it is an aspect of differentiation that often seems unwieldy. One fourth-grade teacher expressed it this way: "I know the

A Differentiation Parallel: From Home to School

My daughter asked, "Is it a problem to fix dinner since I've become a vegetarian?" Giving a crooked smile, I responded, "Well think about it. Dad won't eat carbohydrates, your brother won't eat vegetables, and you don't eat meat. It does pose a few challenges!"

Reflecting later about this brief conversation, I realized my quandary over preparing a family dinner parallels the dilemma of a classroom teacher trying to plan a lesson. My family group was just four in number. What if I had 20 or even 30 diners with distinct needs? What kind of menu would satisfy everyone?

The first bit of counsel I always give to teachers is not to try to do it all. I have to confess that on some days, when it comes to dinnertime, I give my daughter an option of cereal and have let my son bypass the vegetables. For the most part, I strive for balance so all family members can have a healthy meal, but sometimes my solutions are less than ideal—and that's okay, both at the dinner table and in the classroom.

---

content I'm expected to teach and I have the pacing guide I'm required to follow to make sure that *all* of my students move along at the same rate. Then I add my 24 learners clustered into four different reading levels. Just how am I supposed to differentiate?"

Tiered instruction is one way to begin the differentiation journey. Knowing the content, sequence of instruction, and proposed pacing is the first step. Take a moment to think about the following advance organizer to activate your prior knowledge about differentiating through tiered instruction before we add other components.

Each of these statements will be addressed in numerous ways throughout the book. However, rather than have you wonder about these assertions, let's look at them in brief right now.

Know the Curriculum

If you are in a school or school system that does not have established, written curricula, then you can tier instruction based on your individual curriculum and lesson goals. Doing the up-front work of determining what students must know and be able to do as well as having a scope and sequence of how you intend to teach the content will be important.

Advance Organizer: Tiering Instruction

Directions: Read the statements below and mark whether you think they are true or false.

True	False	Statement
T	F	In order for tiered instruction to be successful, students must always work in groups at their achievement levels.
T	F	Scaffolding means providing support at the student's level of need in order for him or her to progress toward new understanding.
T	F	Higher-level, complex thinking can be built into every tier of instruction.
T	F	Leveled textbooks and leveled resource materials should be used by teachers to tier instruction.
T	F	Assessment of student progress should be made weekly.

In order for tiered instruction to be successful, students must always work in groups at their achievement levels. *False.* Many teachers think differentiation means that you must group students by reading levels or test grades. However, in order for tiered instruction to be successful, students do not necessarily have to be grouped with others at the same achievement level. A number of grouping strategies and scenarios are possible, and they will be described in subsequent chapters, but for now keep in mind that using achievement levels is one way to group—but not the only way!

Scaffolding means providing support at the student's level of need in order for him or her to progress toward new understanding. *True.* We use the level of need as a starting point, with the goal of encouraging students to stretch beyond their current independent performance levels. Because a difference exists between what students can do on their own (independent level) and what they can do with help (instructional level), effective instruction requires the teacher to scaffold or adjust the level of support for each learner in response to the student's level of performance. Vygotsky's (1978) zone of proximal development (ZPD) distinguishes between *actual* development—

what students can do on their own—and *potential* development—what students can do with help. Learning is scaffolded for students when a teacher or more competent peer provides hints or prompts to help the learner reach the edge of his or her ZPD through the graduated intervention of the teacher (Greenfield, 1984). We will talk about scaffolding in greater detail in Chapter 2.

Higher-level, complex thinking can be built into every tier of instruction. *True.* All students should participate in complex thinking tasks that involve both critical and creative thinking. Complex, higher-level thinking is not just for the gifted achievers. In fact, relegating struggling students to rote, lower-level question/answer responses impedes their ability to thrive and advance as learners. Examples are provided throughout this book that demonstrate how to probe for thinking at different levels.

Leveled textbooks and leveled resource materials should be used by teachers to tier instruction. *True.* Leveled texts are often seen as tools only to help struggling readers, so you might not think to use them with higher

---

Ways to Use Leveled Texts in Tiered Instruction

Fiction

- Use a variety of leveled fiction books at easier levels to do quick comparisons of setting, characters, plots, conflicts, or themes.

- Use a variety of leveled fiction to practice the skills of prediction, identifying cause and effect, making inferences.

- Use abridged fiction to compare against selected text from the original to analyze the degree to which content is adjusted or eliminated when detail is reduced, and how descriptive vocabulary is adapted or adjusted.

Nonfiction

- Use nonfiction picture books in science, asking students to write in the appropriate text for the picture based on what they have learned in class.

- Use leveled readers to assist students in understanding primary documents, such as asking middle-school students to find the section in the Bill of Rights described in a specific elementary-school leveled reader.

- Ask students to use nonfiction leveled readers as additional resources to complete a study guide on a topic.

---

achievers. However, *leveled* texts can be meaningful tools for *all* learners. In reading, they are especially useful when introducing literary elements or teaching reading strategies because students can focus on the content of the lesson without devoting excessive attention to decoding. Similarly, leveled nonfiction texts frequently offer students a way to absorb content through simpler or more succinct language and graphics.

Assessment of student progress should be made weekly. *False.* Certainly, weekly is better than every other week or five times a grading period; however, the bottom line on assessment is that it should ongoing, constant, never ending—you get the idea!

Ideally assessment informs instruction and helps teachers gain information about student progress by identifying what students know and don't know on various levels. A significant amount of input is gathered automatically, from what you do intuitively on a daily basis. You watch your learners, noting successes and frustrations and informally assess them by observing them, asking questions, and conferencing. You can gather additional insight about student progress through more formal measures, such as tests, quizzes, performances, and products. These informal and formal assessment practices supply you with a wealth of information that helps you design appropriate instruction.

Ready to Begin

Now that you have an overview of the key tenets of tiered instruction, I invite you to examine your own practice to gain insight about where you are on the road to creating a differentiated classroom. Don't worry if you're still a work in progress; everyone is!

Ideas for Reflection

Evidence of Differentiation	Area of Differentiation to Develop

1. Create a T-chart. On the left side write "Evidence of Differentiation." On the right side write "Areas of Differentiation to Develop." Complete this T-chart on your own by writing four to six responses in each column. Compare notes with your colleagues to see if there are similarities or differences in your perspectives.

2. Reflect on your responses to the advanced

A Practical Guide to Tiering Instruction in the Differentiated Classroom © 2010 by Sarah Armstrong, Scholastic Professional

organizer on page 10. Which questions suggest a challenge to teachers as you reflect on ways to design differentiated instruction? Are there areas that are particularly troublesome to you or your colleagues?

3. Use the "10 Tiered Instruction Targets" below as a survey. In what areas are you most confident? In which areas is the most growth needed?

4. In what ways does your team, grade level, or school embrace differentiation?

5. Write a list of all the ways you assess students to gain greater insight about how they are achieving.

Self Assessment: Tiering Instruction

10 Tiered Instruction Targets	I'm there!	I'm making good progress.	I'm trying to move in that direction.
1. I identify the essential understandings that I want students to know.			
2. If you asked the students in my class, they would be able to tell you the goals of the unit.			
3. I pre-assess my students to determine strengths and needs.			
4. I plan the final assessment *before* designing the instruction.			
5. I use assessment to help determine student groupings.			
6. I arrange my groups flexibly; they may vary daily.			
7. I design interesting and relevant lessons to hook and engage the learner.			
8. I create tasks that challenge students and stretch their thinking.			
9. I begin by determining on-level tasks that meet the essential understandings, then I scaffold up or down appropriately for students.			
10. I adjust the complexity, support, pace, materials, and/or directions to meet the needs of learners.			

Chapter 2

Knowing Your Learners: Assessing and Scaffolding to Meet Students' Needs

My friends who are master gardeners tell me that before they turn over any soil in the garden, they spend time making sure that conditions are optimal for the plants they've selected. Though light, water, and the right nutrients are essential for a healthy garden, success also depends on knowing how much sunlight each plant needs, how to space the plants, and at what depth they should be planted. Advance work includes finding out about blooming seasons—researching colors, heights, and the spread of each type of plant—then sketching out a plan to make sure the plants are supported in their natural environment in complementary groupings.

As they make these preparations, master gardeners also note additional accommodations to be made along the way such as fertilizing, trimming, and transplanting. This up-front work and planning helps the garden to thrive. In much the same way, when we think about tiering instruction to help students thrive, what is most critical is the right amount of support at the right time in the right depth, with optimal interaction among peers.

Tiering instruction based on a comprehensive picture of what a teacher knows about each student's achievement, performance, and inclination to learn is akin to a well-thought-out and carefully tended garden. For example, to nurture our students so they achieve their maximum growth, we must discern their reading and math levels, and become aware of their interests and learning style preferences. The way to gain this information is through the use of assessments that provide baseline data at selected points during the year, augmented by frequent and varied assessments. In this chapter, I will discuss a range of assessments that will help you learn more about your individual students and assist you as you plan for differentiated instruction.

Though assessment will be discussed in further detail in Chapter 6, some of the pre-assessments and student self-evaluation tools that inform lesson planning are discussed here. The practice of differentiating instruction is founded on the belief that all students can learn and that our job as teachers is to establish the culture that allows learning to take place. In effect, you are the master gardener in your classroom, responsible for doing the up-front work so your students can take root and bloom.

Assessing Reading Levels

When it comes to differentiation using tiered content, it is important to note that the difficulty of the text is one of the first barriers that struggling learners encounter in a classroom. Even students who make an effort to get the content from the textbook will give up if it seems too dense or there are too many unfamiliar vocabulary words. You've seen some of these avoidance techniques: head on the desk, staring at a book pretending to read, acting-out behaviors such as talking out, slamming books, hostility toward you or other students, and declarations such as, *This is dumb! Who needs this stuff! When will I ever use this? I don't get it. It's too hard!*

Getting a handle on your students' instructional reading levels is a basic first step in tiering instruction because we must provide texts and other materials students can read. I know of a number of elementary and middle schools where Informal Reading Inventories (IRI) are given to any child suspected of reading below grade level. Some schools survey students' reading levels with other effective reading assessments. Regardless of how students are assessed, having a fix on the level at which a student reads text independently, as well as on his or her instructional reading level, will allow you to secure the materials necessary to differentiate instruction for your particular group.

The following reading assessments are among the many tools available to teachers as they examine students' literacy development. Additional information can be found at the Web sites provided.

Resources for Reading Assessments

Reading Assessment	Grades	Web Site
Dynamic Indicators of Basic Early Literacy Skills, 6th Edition (DIBELS–6)	Pre-K, K–3	https://dibels.uoregon.edu/
Developmental Reading Assessment, K–3, 2nd Edition (DRA-2, K–3)	K, 1, 2, 3	http://www.pearsonschool.com/
Phonological Awareness Literacy Screening—1–3 (PALS-1–3)	1, 2, 3	http://pals.virginia.edu/
Analytical Reading Inventory, 8th Edition	K, 1, 2, 3, and higher	http://www.mypearsonstore.com/bookstore/product.asp?isbn=0131568086
Diagnostic Assessments of Reading, 2nd Edition	K, 1, 2, 3, and higher	http://www.riversidepublishing.com/
Qualitative Reading Inventory, 4th Edition (QRI-4)	K, 1, 2, 3, and higher	http://www.directtextbook.com/9780205443277/qualitative-reading-inventory-4-4th-leslie-0205443273
STAR Reading Computer-Adaptive Reading Test	K, 1, 2, 3, and higher	http://www.renlearn.com/
Scholastic Reading Inventory (SRI)	K–12	http://teacher.scholastic.com/products/sri_reading_assessment/programoverview.htm

The Role of Assessment in the Differentiated Classroom

Once you have a grasp of reading levels, the next step is to think about the process you go through as you design a lesson and monitor student progress. As a teacher, you constantly ask yourself, "What do my students need to know and how do I know if they know it?" This question assumes that

A Practical Guide to Tiering Instruction in the Differentiated Classroom © 2010 by Sarah Armstrong, Scholastic Professional

A Classroom Assessment System

"Today, more teachers are thinking about assessment in their classrooms as a balanced system of components. One component, **summative assessment**, fulfills the traditional role of measuring student progress. Results from tests feed into an evaluation, like a mark in a grade book or a report card grade. Also known as assessments of learning, they reflect the level of student learning at a particular point in time.

Another component, **formative assessment**, is an ongoing process used to inform instructional decisions made by the teacher and student. This process can be extended to encourage and promote further learning. Formative assessments, linked to the targets of daily instruction, provide continuous information . . . as opposed to a summative snapshot. Formative assessment happens while teaching is still under way, helping shape decisions about what needs to happen next to better prepare students for the summative assessment.

In a balanced classroom assessment system, neither of these two components is over- or underused; they work together to generate the combined effects that are greater than the sum of the individual parts. When summative and formative classroom assessments are high quality and purposefully planned, they are synergistic parts of the same system and can help form a more complete and accurate picture of student learning." (Chappuis & Stiggins, 2008, p. 12)

assessment and teaching are inseparable—and in fact they are. Because of this interdependence, Wiggins and McTighe (1998) emphasize the importance of backward design—or what they call "beginning with the end in mind." Specifically, a teacher needs to know the knowledge, skills, and understandings that will be assessed and determine the method of assessment *before* students are taught. With backward design, the teacher has clarity about both what students must learn and how it will be measured. Using this approach, there should be few surprises for students when it comes to test time.

Assessment *for* Learning

The difference between didactic teaching to the test and instructional practices that develop students as learners and thinkers is captured in the distinction between assessment *of* learning and assessment *for* learning. Differentiated instruction necessitates the second approach to assessment. Rather than "teaching to the test," which is called assessment *of* learning, we strive to support students as they grow as learners, using assessment *for* learning to guide our teaching. Assessment *for* learning is much richer than traditional assessments, taking into account the learner as a whole person and influencing not only grades, but how we teach and what we ask students to do. Assessment *for* learning occurs throughout the entire lesson or unit of study, not just at the end.

Richard Stiggins (2005), lead consultant at the Assessment Training Institute, highlights five categories of achievement targets that support thinking about assessment for learning:

- knowledge
- reasoning
- performance skills
- products
- dispositions

Only one of these five achievement types—knowledge—is readily assessed by multiple-choice tests. Most benchmark tests, end-of-course tests, and year-end comprehensive assessments measure discrete facts and information that students have been taught because they are "on the test." To truly help students progress as learners, however, teachers must also use assessment tools that measure reasoning, performance skills, and the quality of student products.

From a student's point of view, tests that measure knowledge answer a single question: "Did I pass or did I fail?" As a result, they often find assessment stressful and frequently unrewarding. Since how students feel about taking a test can influence the results, we particularly need to pay attention to another category on Stiggins's list—*dispositions*—which includes attitudes, interests, and motivational intentions of our students. When we assess disposition, we ask students how they feel about the learning experience and determine the degree to which they are motivated by what we are asking them to do. Assessing disposition keys into how well a student likes or dislikes the subject and/or instructional approaches. Sometimes students have a reasonable grasp of content but freeze on certain kinds of tests or in particular testing situations. Knowing the disposition of the student can help you make the appropriate accommodations. The surveys on pages 19 and 20 illustrate ways to tap into students' dispositions in pre- and post-assessment situations.

A Practical Guide to Tiering Instruction in the Differentiated Classroom © 2010 by Sarah Armstrong, Scholastic Professional

Pre-Assessment of Project Preferences

Dear Students:

During this grading period, we will have two projects. Before we get into these assignments, I would like to know some of your preferences when it comes to completing projects. Your responses to the following statements will help me. Please check option 1, 2, or 3 for each one. Thank you.

Statement		Option 1		Option 2		Option 3
I prefer completing a project:	☐	by myself	☐	with one other person	☐	with a small group
When it comes to selecting a topic:	☐	give me the guidelines and I would like to select my own.	☐	let me select from several options you provide.	☐	assign a topic to me.
When it comes to organization:	☐	I need a written timeline and would like you to check with me often along the way.	☐	I need a written timeline and would like you to look at my final draft.	☐	just tell me when it is due and give me the project expectations. I will have it done.
I prefer the following method of presentation:	☐	using SMART Board and PowerPoint	☐	incorporating art, mixed media, and music	☐	completing a written report and oral presentation.
When it comes to finding resources:	☐	I have ready access to computer, Internet, and library resources on my own.	☐	I have access to a computer but can only get on the Internet at school.	☐	I will need to use the computer and other resources at school.

Dear Students:

I want to get your input about how this class has gone for you during this grading period. I will use your response to help me prepare for the next nine weeks. Please candidly respond to the prompts below. You will **not** need to include your name on this survey.

The best part of class during these nine weeks has been:

The content that I found most interesting was:

The content that I am still struggling to understand better is:

If one thing could be changed about this class, I would suggest:

One thing about this class I would not change is:

I would like to have more of the following (check any that apply):

___ cooperative group work   ___ self-assessment

___ choices about whom I work with   ___ "Look for" notes that detail what is expected

___ opportunities to use technology   ___ independent study

___ resources other than the textbook   ___ partner projects

Please feel free to make additional comments on the back of this page.

A Range of Assessments

Teachers in differentiated classrooms find the path easier to negotiate if they embrace a broader conception of assessment. The key is to include a wide range of assessment tools to help guide your thinking about student performance and achievement as you move through a lesson or unit of study. With ongoing assessment, you have the information needed to provide appropriate scaffolding every step of the way. As previously noted, when planning lessons it is important to begin with the end in mind. When you have the end in mind, you know where you want to go, and assessments provide the road map for the journey.

Your range of assessment tools should include specific feedback and self-assessment, which may be delivered as pre-assessments or as diagnostic assessments along the way. One strategy for pre-assessment is to consider the essential understandings for a particular unit and then develop a way to measure these understandings. The pre-assessment might double as the final unit assessment. By designing the assessment before teaching the unit, you are planning with the end in mind. A pre-assessment should be given in plenty of time to make adjustments in instructional plans (i.e., at least a week in advance). The value of pre-assessment becomes clear when we consider the range of information it provides (McTighe & O'Connor, 2005):

- What to teach: What skill gaps should I address? What material may I skip because it was previously mastered?

- How to teach: How should I group my students? What are the students' preferred learning styles? How can I connect the information to students' interests and strengths?

Pre-assessments are essential as teachers make decisions about selecting text material, arranging learning groups, or determining how students will demonstrate their knowledge.

> *"One of the realities is that, while all students can learn, they will not all start at the same place, learn at the same rate, or reach the same ultimate level of proficiency. This is because of differences in academic ability, interests, and commitments. The perfect assessment system will accommodate these by providing a continuous-progress curriculum and then by relying on assessment, record keeping, and communication processes that provide accurate information that adjusts to student needs."*
>
> *(Chappuis et al., 2005, p. 29)*

Self-Assessment of Learning

Students' self-assessment is valuable for pre-assessment as well as at various points throughout the lesson or unit you're teaching. When students have clear criteria to review and are asked to reflect on the degree to which *they* think they meet stated expectations, they gain a better grasp of the instructional targets they are moving toward. In many classrooms, indicators framed with "I can" statements are provided to students as a way to involve them in self-assessment. The following survey of students with regard to their thinking skills

---

Sample Self-Assessment

Student Name: _____ Date: _____

Self-Assessment on the Build It 3-D Unit

Skills in Build It 3-D	*Very Confident*	*Somewhat Confident*	*Still Need Help*
I can use a protractor.			
I can find the sum of angles, triangles, and quadrilaterals.			
I can explain when and why shapes are congruent.			
I can sort triangles and quadrilaterals.			
I can name 2-D figures from drawings.			
I can correctly associate a prefix in a name with a number.			
I can identify lines of symmetry.			
I can classify triangles by side lengths and angle measurements.			
I can draw polygons.			
I can identify three attributes for any polygon.			

Assessment developed by Rosina P. Headley

is an example of a self-assessment that guides students to consider their own thinking and provides valuable information to teachers.

Self-assessment can be accomplished using an array of strategies. As noted in Chapter 1, advance organizers can be used to elicit what students know or think they know. A more informal approach is to ask students to do a "quick write" in their journal on everything they can recall about a particular topic. For example, a teacher beginning a unit on the American Revolution might tell students that they have two minutes to write down any word, phrase, or piece of information they can think of that has to do with the American Revolution and the colonists' fight for independence. In this case, the strategy serves as a tool to activate prior knowledge.

A quick write can also be used to review content at the end of a class period. For instance, after a teacher finishes a lesson on natural, human, and capital resources, she might tell her students: *I am going to ask you to do a two-minute quick write on the content of today's lesson. Please write down in your science journal anything you can recall related to natural, human, and capital resources—and make sure I can read it!*

With continuous assessment, teachers regularly check for understanding at the end of a lesson—referred to as closure. These closure or exit activities are used to communicate both what students learned and any questions they might have about the content. An excellent strategy to get students to self-assess is illustrated in the following "3, 2, 1" technique.

3, 2, 1 Exit Activity

Student: _____

1. Write down three things you learned today.

2. Write down two ways that what you learned today is connected to "real life."

3. Write down one question you have or one area you would like me to review tomorrow.

Tracking Results

An essential step in maximizing the use of a variety of assessments is to develop a system to track the results. This may be done in a number of ways, such as a checklist of standards, a handwritten list of student needs, or a matrix of results. Students may also track their own progress by setting a goal, determining tasks to meet the goal, and examining results. Checklists, rubrics, or a student-plotted line graph might be ways to encourage students to track progress. The matrix below identifies student progress on the geometry skills mentioned earlier. A check means the student has mastered the skill. You will note that this format provides a helpful at-a-glance record detailing which students need additional support.

Sample Matrix for Tracking Assessment Results

Classroom Checklist for Build It 3-D

Skills in Build It 3-D	Mikayla	Ally	Emily	Faith	Megan	Karie	Austin	Ryan	Luke	Hayden	John	Kelley	Mikey
1. Use of protractor		✓					✓	✓		✓	✓		✓
2. Angle sums of triangles and quadrilaterals		✓	✓				✓	✓	✓	✓	✓	✓	✓
3. Congruency	✓	✓	✓	✓			✓	✓	✓	✓		✓	✓
4. Sorting triangles and quadrilaterals	✓	✓	✓	✓	✓	✓	✓	✓	✓	✓	✓	✓	✓
5. Naming 2-D figures from drawings	✓	✓	✓				✓	✓	✓	✓	✓	✓	✓
6. Association of a prefix in a name with a number	✓	✓	✓	✓	✓	✓	✓	✓	✓	✓	✓	✓	✓
7. Lines of symmetry		✓	✓		✓		✓	✓	✓			✓	✓
8. Classifying triangles by side lengths or angle measurements	✓	✓	✓	✓	✓	✓	✓	✓	✓	✓	✓	✓	✓
9. Classifying quadrilaterals through pairs of parallel sides	✓				✓		✓	✓	✓	✓		✓	
10. Drawing polygons	✓	✓	✓	✓		✓	✓	✓		✓	✓	✓	✓
11. Three attributes for any polygon		✓	✓		✓					✓	✓		
12. Regular polygons versus irregular polygons		✓				✓	✓	✓	✓	✓	✓	✓	

Ongoing Assessment

A fifth-grade lead teacher presenting formative assessment strategies to her colleagues calls it the "never-ending story." She adds, "Wouldn't it be nice if teachers could have an assessment checklist, and once something was checked off, it was done!" The following stages of assessment (adapted from Ainsworth & Viegut, 2006, p. 25) illustrate the point she was making:

Stage one: Pre-assess → Analyze results → Plan for differentiation

Stage two: Teach → Monitor/reflect/adjust → Teach

Stage three: Post-assess

Without a doubt, assessment is cyclical. Examining student performance and identifying areas of improvement are tasks that teachers do on a daily basis. The key to differentiation is knowing where to go next following both pre-assessment and post-assessment. In fact, the ability to diagnose and prescribe where students need to go next is at the heart of differentiation. This knowledge allows you to identify and provide the scaffolding students need to move ahead.

Scaffolding: The Link Between Assessment and Instruction

Most of us have watched young children take their first steps. Practice starts with Mom, Dad, or big sibling holding both hands, so there is no potential for falling. When a baby takes those first few steps independently, everything goes smoothly for two or three steps, and then the baby gets wobbly and plops down on a well-padded backside.

Scaffolding needs to occur at the place where the learner gets wobbly. Scaffolding, which is directly tied to Vygotsky's zone of proximal development, is described as "what teachers say or do to enable children to complete complex mental tasks they could not complete without assistance" (Pearson & Fielding, 1991, as cited in Hogan & Pressley, 1997, p. 41). When a student is no longer able to progress at a task on his or her own, and assistance or support is needed, skillful teaching becomes essential. Scaffolding occurs when you listen to students, assess and acknowledge their individual strengths, and coach and prod them into a deeper level of understanding.

> ## *Scaffolding at a Glance*
>
> When planning tiered lessons, keep these guidelines for scaffolding in mind:
>
> - Know the learners and evaluate their particular needs.
>
> - Make independent learning the goal.
>
> - Keep in mind the student's zone of proximal development (ZPD) by assessing the point at which a student no longer manages on his or her own and support is needed.
>
> - Break tasks into smaller, more manageable parts.
>
> - Keep the learner in pursuit of the task while minimizing the learner's stress level
>
> - Only offer assistance with skills beyond the student's capability. If students are able to do the work, insist that they do. Give just enough assistance to overcome the current obstacle.
>
> - Ensure frequent success, which increases motivation through a positive self-efficacy
>
> - Begin the process of "fading," gradually removing scaffolding when the student assumes responsibility.
>
> - Remove scaffolding completely when mastery of the task is demonstrated.
>
> As Hogan and Pressley (1997) note, scaffolding includes "recruiting the student's interest, reducing the number of steps so the task is manageable, maintaining student's persistence toward the goal, making critical features evident, and controlling frustration and risk" (p. 47).

Assessing by Tuning In to What Students Know and What They Don't

A key tenet of scaffolding is that teachers must listen for and observe student responses and questions. Many times these fertile assessment opportunities are bypassed because a teacher gives the answer or fills in the silence before a student responds. Following class visits, I often ask teachers, "Who was doing the work of learning in your classroom, you or the students?" I ask this question because I want teachers to reflect deeply on the degree to which responsibility for learning is pushed back onto the student—not as receptacles of information, but as participants! For example, while observing a teacher in a history class on the topic of population demographics, a student asked, "What does the word *dominance* mean?" Without even a split-second delay, the teacher defined the word for the student. I sighed, because to me that moment was an opportunity to assess where the student was coming from and get the student—and perhaps the whole class—to think. The teacher could have made a number of other choices by turning the question back to the student, involving other students in the response, or setting up a scenario that would provide more information to help clarify the word. Immediate responses could have been:

- Do you have thoughts about what it might mean?

- Are there several of you in class who could give examples—not a definition, but examples—in different contexts?

- If I said that the choice of pizza has dominance over chicken nuggets every day in the cafeteria, does that give you an idea? What comes to mind then?

When instruction is scaffolded, teachers seldom provide the answers; rather, they construct the opportunities for students to retrieve, uncover, discover, and arrive at the responses themselves.

> *"Scaffolding is used in a very wide range of situations. Mothers naturally employ this approach as they teach their children how to live in and enjoy their world. Teachers, from pre-K to adult education appreciate the necessity and increased learning afforded by the use of these techniques. Non-traditional educational settings, such as business-training scenarios and athletic teams, also use these methods to assure the success of their employees and/or members."*
>
> —Lipscomb, Swanson, & West, 2004

The Management of Scaffolding

Teachers agree that scaffolding is necessary to move learners along; however, figuring out how to scaffold efficiently is often another story. But when you conduct ongoing assessment and know precisely where your students wobble, you can be ready to provide the instructional support they need.

A key facilitator in managing scaffolding is organizing students in work groups to the extent possible (Hogan & Pressley, 1997). This allows you to scaffold with four or five groups as opposed to 25 individual students. One tool you can use to help you group students is the Student Scaffolding Readiness Scale (see example on page 28 and template on page 138), which will help you assess entry levels of students prior to teaching a specific unit of study. The scale encompasses four key areas that inform you about ways to differentiate for students:

- **Background Knowledge:** Making connections between the new and known is essential. Insufficient background knowledge is a significant reason for achievement delays, and students with more limited vocabularies are disadvantaged in their ability to comprehend and develop as writers.

- **Higher-Order Thinking:** Students need to see models and practice higher-order thinking skills. As students gain facility in tackling complex thinking and problem solving, their persistence on tasks improves as well as their comprehension.

- **Interaction With Content:** In assessing when and how to scaffold, teachers must make decisions about the level of text or resources to use and the pace at which a student can progress.

- **Degree of Independence:** When a student's degree of independence and confidence increases when tackling new learning tasks, he or she is more likely ready to scaffold to the next level.

You can use this tool to plan activities and group students, as we see in the following examples.

Student Scaffolding Readiness Scale

Student : _____   Teacher: _____   Grade: _____   Date:_____

Category	Degree of Readiness									
Background Knowledge	1	2	3	4	5	6	7	8	9	10
• Familiarity with the content	Unfamiliar									Very familiar
• Related background knowledge	Limited or none									Substantial experience
• Vocabulary	Mostly unfamiliar									Strong grasp of essential and related vocabulary
• Reading Level	Two or more years below									Confidently above level
Evidence of Higher-Order Thinking	1	2	3	4	5	6	7	8	9	10
• Capacity to handle choice with task	Needs guidance									Performs without direction
• Complexity of thinking	Knowing Understanding Applying									Analyzing Evaluating Creating
• Facility with abstract material	Initially needs concrete, tangible evidence									Works well with abstract examples
Interaction With Content	1	2	3	4	5	6	7	8	9	10
• Skill level	Entry									Mastery
• Ability to handle pacing of lesson	Additional time needed									Content can be compacted for acceleration
• Scope of resources used	Needs leveled readers and supplemental materials									Needs access to enrichment resources
• Level of direction needed	Step by step strong support of teacher									Overview only with intermittent checks
Degree of Independence	1	2	3	4	5	6	7	8	9	10
• The degree to which modeling is needed	Dependent on teacher									Independent
• The degree to which practice is needed	Needs built-in practice with ongoing feedback									Can move to enrichment quickly
• The degree to which rehearsal is needed	Must teach/assess/reteach									Minimal rehearsal needed

A Practical Guide to Tiering Instruction in the Differentiated Classroom © 2010 by Sarah Armstrong, Scholastic Professional

ONE TEACHER'S USE OF THE STUDENT
SCAFFOLDING READINESS SCALE

Mr. Faber was beginning a new unit of study with his fifth-grade class. He planned to use nonfiction leveled readers and connect his reading instruction to his science instruction. The content to be learned pertained to plate tectonics:

- The earth's heat energy causes movement of material within the earth. Continent-size blocks (plates) move slowly about the earth's surface, driven by that heat.

- Most earthquakes and volcanoes are located at the boundary of the plates (faults). Plates can move together (convergent boundaries), apart (divergent boundaries), or slip past each other horizontally (sliding boundaries, also called strike-slip or transform boundaries).

- Geological features in the oceans (including trenches and mid-ocean ridges) and on the continents (mountain ranges) are caused by current and past plate movements. (Source: Virginia DOE, 2003)

Mr. Faber decided to use the readiness scale to determine how to group his 26 students. Although he had an idea of the spectrum of student achievement, he thought it would be purposeful at the beginning of a new grading period to use the scale to reflect on each student. He had asked students to do a quick-write pre-assessment on plate tectonics and had reviewed responses in their science notebooks to get some idea of their background knowledge. After looking at the results of the completed readiness scales, he determined the following:

- Six students were reading below grade level. Four of the six were students who needed a great deal of direction and support. These six learners had a significant lack of background knowledge about plate tectonics.

- Sixteen students had similar responses and a general sense of related terminology at a basic level. Six of the sixteen were above-grade readers. Ten of the sixteen were on-grade readers with three students who did not work well independently and needed significant monitoring by the teacher.

- Four students had a high level of background knowledge as evidenced by the extent of the vocabulary and terms cited. They were above-grade readers, and three of the four were very capable of handling a great deal of choice and complexity of material.

Student Scaffolding Readiness Scale Summary

(Scores of 1, 2, or 3 are areas to be developed and are noted as "D"; scores of 8, 9, and 10 are areas of strength and are noted as "S")

Teacher: _____   Grade: _____   Period: _____   Date: _____   Content: Plate Tectonics Unit

Category	Angie	Brian	Caleb	Carrie	Dawson	Ellie	Fran	Freddie	Gail	Harper	India	Jaleel	Jeremy	Lauren	Montana	Noelle	Paul	Reggie	Robbie	Serena	Stanley	Thomas	Valerie	Will	Yancy	Zeb
Background Knowledge																										
• Familiarity with the content	S		D			D					D					S		D			D				D	S
• Related background knowledge			D			D					D					S		D		S	D				D	S
• Vocabulary	S		D			D					D					S		D	S	S	D				D	S
• Reading level	S		D			D	S				D		S			S		D	S	S	D	S			D	S
Evidence of Higher-Order Thinking																										
• Capacity to handle choice with task			D			D					D					S		D							D	S
• Complexity of thinking			D								D					S				S	D					S
• Facility with abstract material	S		D								D					S				S	D				D	S
Interaction With Content																										
• Skill level	S															S				S		S				S
• Ability to handle pacing of lesson	S	D											D			S				S		S				S
• Scope of resources used																S				S						S
• Level of direction needed	S	D											D			S						S				S
Degree of Independence																										
• Modeling is needed			D		D						D							D							D	
• Practice is needed			D		D						D							D							D	
• Rehearsal is needed			D		D						D							D							D	

Mr. Faber divided his class into four groups, taking into consideration reading levels and persistence with independent activities. When completing the summary form, he was particularly interested in the students who were at the lowest ends of the Readiness Scale with 1, 2, or 3 (noted with a D, for "Development" needed) and the students at the highest ends with 8, 9, or 10 (noted with an S, for "Strength" in that area). Mr. Faber recognized that these students likely needed additional support or enrichment. He used a range of leveled readers in each group and differentiated the assignment based on these factors. He also created a rubric to assess their performance. Specific examples of differentiation by these criteria will be provided in later chapters.

Mr. Faber decided to build his groups as follows:

Group 1	Group 2	Group 3	Group 4
The emphasis is on connecting to background knowledge and clarifying vocabulary terms using many visual prompts. Numerous nonfiction materials at instructional reading levels are provided with strong teacher coaching.	The emphasis is on building on existing knowledge of plate tectonics. Nonfiction materials at a range of levels are provided. The teacher models thinking and sets up tasks that reinforce the content. The teacher coaches and monitors progress of students.	The emphasis is on providing numerous resources that affirm and enhance basic knowledge. A range of tasks that build connections are provided with student choices built in. Students may work independently or with a partner. The teacher serves as a resource.	The emphasis is on broadening access to resources at many levels and expanding vocabulary and connections. Students define and identify real-life topics to be explored and work with a partner or small group. The teacher serves as a resource.
Caleb	Brian	Carrie	Angie
India	Dawson	Fran	Noelle
Reggie	Jaleel	Jeremy	Serena
Stanley	Gail	Montana	Zeb
Yancy	Harper	Lauren	Thomas
	Ellie	Paul	Robbie
		Valerie	Freddie
		Will	

Taking the Next Step

After analyzing the levels of students, cluster them into smaller work groups geared to meeting the learning goals of the unit. Once the results of completed scales have been examined, you can consider the following questions:

- What are the likely misunderstandings or errors?

- How can I redirect students if the content is too difficult? Too simple?

- At what point do I think the student will *wobble*?

- How can I provide the instruction to take students to the next level?

This readiness tool could be used once or twice during a grading period or even more frequently, serving as the basis for a variety of groupings. For example, with a classroom of 26 students, a group of 15 might be clustered at the beginning of a new unit to develop background knowledge and build related vocabulary. Within that group, some of the students may quickly gain independence and move to more complex tasks, while others will remain in a smaller group that requires more support. Conceivably, after two lessons, students may be structured into three groups: 1) highly independent, 2) somewhat independent with practice necessary, and 3) dependent with ongoing feedback and support needed. The Student Scaffolding Readiness Scale can assist in planning for differentiated groupings and tiered instruction on a variety of fronts.

Insight on Flexible Tiered Groups

- Be flexible. As Wormeli notes, "There won't always be high, medium, and low tiers. Respond to the unique characteristics of the students in front of you instead of imposing a predetermined leveling" (2007, p. 57).

- Many examples illustrate tiering using three groups. However, this is *not* a defined number. Three groups show how you might begin with an engaging activity and then scaffold up or down based on the needs of students. There may be times when you will have only two groups—those that are on level and those that need support. There may be times when you will have more than three groups—when there are more identified levels or needs within tasks. The key is to consider what is manageable. It is best to begin small and feel comfortable in meeting with all groups and providing adequate support.

Feedback as Part of the Assessment Picture

The purpose of feedback is to inform students about their learning and to advance them to a new level. W. James Popham, author of *Transformative Assessment* (2008), emphasizes the importance of descriptive feedback which indicates what students can do currently and what they need to do to attain a target or learning goal. He states, "Empirical research tells us that such feedback is far more effective in improving student learning than comparative feedback, in which a student receives only an assessment-based grade or class ranking" (p. 114).

Feedback is powerful when it encourages students to reflect. "To be effective, feedback needs to cause thinking. Grades don't do that. Scores don't do that. And comments like 'good job' don't do that either. What does cause thinking is a comment that addresses what the student needs to do to improve, linked to rubrics where appropriate" (Leahy, Lyon, Thompson, & William, 2008, p. 24). Characteristics of quality feedback include four criteria (Wiggins, 1998). Feedback must be:

- Timely
- Specific
- Understandable to the student
- Communicated in such a way that it guides the student so she or he can self-adjust

The purpose of effective feedback is to help students see where they wobbled, facilitate new understanding, and push them to the next level. A meaningful feedback system helps learners know what they have done well and what they can do the next time to improve. An essential step in providing feedback is to also give students the chance to "refine, revise, practice, and retry" (McTighe & O'Connor, 2005, p. 13). In one school I visited, teachers used a "glow and grow" system to provide feedback on student work. Each project or writing task had a *glow* response, such as "I like the way you use descriptive adverbs to set the mood of the story." A *grow* response for the same paper was, "Remember to expand your use of verbs. Why don't you make a list of verbs that can replace the word *ran*?" Another teacher's *glow* comment for a project was, "I like the connection you made between the story and your life" while her *grow* comment was, "Remember to stick closely to the rubric for guidelines on how to organize the project."

Think of constructive feedback that you have received. If you have taken tennis lessons, you listen carefully to the coach's suggestions for elevating your game. As a member of a 16-voice a cappella group, I, along with the other 15 singers, regularly receive specific feedback from the director on phrasing, blend, and dynamics. We listen to the feedback because it results—almost immediately—in a higher quality of performance. Without a doubt feedback guides actions, changes focus, and influences learning. Effective feedback is critical in the effort to scaffold students to the next level.

Summary

I recently watched a mother coach her young daughter about crossing the street. She said, "You need to stop, look, and listen. Stop before moving forward. Look all around you for traffic, and listen for anything coming your way." I think this is the crux of assessment. As teachers we stop before we move ahead instructionally and look at student achievement through a wide range of assessments. Using these assessments we listen, discerning how to scaffold students to the next level. In Chapter 3, we transition from assessment and scaffolding to differentiated lesson design.

Ideas for Reflection

1. Consider the students in your classes. What are their dispositions (attitudes and feelings) about assessment? To what degree do their dispositions influence their success in your classes?

2. As a self-assessment, design a survey that would give you feedback from students indicating how they feel about their success in your classroom. Ask a colleague to give the survey to his or her classes and discuss the results. Are there areas that are particularly troublesome to you or your colleague?

3. Use the Student Scaffolding Readiness Scale with a class or group of students. How does it inform your planning for instruction? How will it influence your grouping? Share your results with a colleague.

4. Reflect on your system of providing powerful feedback to students. Are there areas in which you feel you provide feedback more effectively (such as projects, journals) than others?

5. Why is activating prior knowledge (APK) an essential part of a powerful lesson?

Chapter 3

Lesson Design With Tiering in Mind

Now that you have an overview of the connection between differentiation and assessment, including the importance of knowing the reading levels and dispositions of the students in your class, it's time to turn our attention to designing lessons that will engage and support your learners. Tiered instruction can energize learning for students across all achievement levels. However, before elaborating further on tiered instruction, I want to discuss the components of outstanding lesson design that are the foundation of a high-quality lesson—tiered or not. In short, a tiered lesson is only valuable if it reflects best practice in lesson design.

A beginning premise is that you have a clear understanding of the facts and concepts in the curriculum, including the designated standard or competency to be taught and the big ideas related to the standard. Many school districts have a designated curriculum for each grade level that teachers must follow. The curriculum often comprises specific standards of learning or competencies that students must meet. Frequently, both the sequence and pacing of the content are outlined. One place to look for this information is on the department of education Web site for your state. Some school districts or schools follow curriculum guides that are developed by grade-level teams, departments, or individual teachers. Typically, these guides outline the content and suggest pacing for lesson planning. In other situations, schools may have specific textbooks that provide a scope and sequence for the course to guide teacher planning.

Once you are clear about the content to be taught, keep these four things in mind as you plan your lessons:

- Plan how you will assess student progress through multiple measures, including pre-assessment and student self-assessment; use this information to adjust your lesson as necessary (as discussed in the previous chapter).

- Activate prior knowledge in a way that captures the attention of the learner.

Reeling in Learners

"I love to fish—from deep sea to mountain stream and everything in between, so let's see what fishing might have to show us about differentiation based on your students' needs. Imagine sitting in a boat on a lake on a warm day, casting a fishing pole into the beautiful sunrise. What are you fishing for and  what bait are you using? Are you fishing with night crawlers next to a shallow bank for sunfish or bream? Are you jigging a live minnow on a deeper brush pile for a school of crappies? Are you resting heavily scented chicken livers on the bottom for a catfish? Are you casting lures into the grass beds and other structures for a largemouth bass? Notice how in each of these examples, the bait on the hook is different based on the 'audience.' In our classrooms, the student audience is always our first consideration when planning lessons. What will hook your students; what are their interests and their background understandings? Once you've answered these questions, you are better equipped to capture the attention of your learners!"

— Stephanie Haskins

- Organize your lesson in chunks of time so students stay tuned in.
- Use strategies (including guided practice) that will engage learners in work that is meaningful, authentic, and supportive of the concepts and facts being taught.

Activating Prior Knowledge: Strategies for Reeling in Learners

Activating prior knowledge (APK) is an essential component of lesson design, a fact corroborated by what we know about the brain and learning. The phrase "neurons that fire together, wire together" explains it best. As students confront new content, their brains search for existing neurons with which to connect the new information (firing), in turn reinforcing synaptic growth and helping to make the learning permanent (wiring). Activating prior knowledge is crucial because when new information is hooked onto what students already know, it prepares their brains to learn.

The importance of APK in lesson design is not a recent finding. More than 25 years ago, Madeline Hunter, distinguished researcher and author on mastery teaching, highlighted the importance of what she called *anticipatory* set. She mentions getting the attention of students with a hook, and asserts that activation of prior knowledge will set up the organizing framework for the ideas, concepts, and information that follow (Hunter, 1984). Students will be better able to follow the flow of instruction because the connections they make during APK primes their brains for the lesson. Similarly, schema theory informs us that what we remember is influenced by what we know and that memories are reconstructed by connecting current experience with prior knowledge. Schemas incorporate both facts that have been taught and generalizations from personal experience. When new content is taught, the connections fall into place, influencing expectations about what is to be learned and helping learners interpret the current input (Driscoll, 2005). If you don't help students make these connections, students give you the "I don't get it" look. In fact, your learners may have the potential, but the schema was never activated.

Providing a Powerful APK Experience

Taking time for a quality APK activity reaps great rewards. Let's look at some of the attributes of activating prior knowledge by examining weak and strong models of APK. Below are some of the factors to consider.

Activating prior knowledge is not simply a three-minute process during which the teacher asks a few questions and a few students respond. When doing an APK strategy with students, rather than asking them to verbally give

Key Factors in Developing Effective APK Activities

With Regard to	Weak APK	Strong APK
Teacher Role	Director: didactic teaching; teacher as expert	Facilitator: coaching responses through questions
Number of Students Responding	A few students, typically the first to raise hands	All students
Reflection of Students	Quick response to a "Who can remember?" question	Thoughtful response to a prompt with time to process information
Levels of Thinking	Knowledge, Comprehension (Bloom)	Application, Analysis, Evaluation, Synthesis (Bloom)
Modalities Used	Scatter questioning—asks the whole class and takes a few responses	Uses visual prompts, journal self-reflection, partner interaction
Connections to Real Life	Some connections by a few respondents	Purposeful questioning to make content relevant to all learners
Student Engagement	Some connections by a few respondents	All students engaged using various modalities and peer interaction

A Practical Guide to Tiering Instruction in the Differentiated Classroom © 2010 by Sarah Armstrong, Scholastic Professional

back things they know about a topic, get them to discuss not only *what* but *how* they know the information. Discussion and even debate result in greater conceptual understanding (Guzzetti, Snyder, Glass, & Gamas, 1993). Consider the following two approaches to activating prior knowledge in fifth-grade social studies classes and think about which one provides a richer experience and builds more connections.

Scenario 1

Teacher: Today we will be starting a unit on the conditions in the states following the Civil War. It was a period of time referred to as Reconstruction. What do you think of when you hear the word *Reconstruction*?

Max: It must mean that something was torn down because it has to be constructed again.

Teacher: Thank you, Max. Who has another thought?

Sophie: When a tree fell on our house in the storm, we had to reconstruct the garage roof.

Teacher: Good connection. Can someone else give me an idea?

Reggie: When things are broken, like my little brother breaks my toys, I try to put them back together. Isn't that reconstruction?

Teacher: All these ideas tell us something about *Reconstruction*. Turn to page 128 in your book and let's get some more information.

Scenario 2

Teacher: I want to show you several photographs from cities and towns that were taken during and right after the Civil War. While I do that I will give you 90 seconds to write down descriptive words or phrases that come to mind when you see the pictures.

Teacher: Now, I want you to share with one or two people next to you the words you just wrote and see if you can add new ones to your own list. You have 90 seconds.

Teacher: Tell me some of the words you came up with, and I will write them on this chart.

Students: *Destruction, ruin, bombed out, death, abandoned, lonely, hungry, poor, wounded, broken, destroyed, help, sad, homeless, hopeful, lost, start over.*

Teacher: So . . . here's my question. Why is the period right after the Civil War referred to as "Reconstruction"? Using what you know and additional information you might have gathered from the pictures, talk to your neighbor(s) and come up with as many areas as you can that you think needed reconstructing. You have two minutes. *(After two minutes)* I would like five ideas from your partner discussion to write on the board. Who will start?

Teacher: Here's a follow-up question. Have there been times in your lives when a period of "reconstruction" has existed either personally for you or in our country or world? You have 30 seconds of think time. *(After 30 seconds)* Would anyone like to share their thoughts?

Let's talk about the two APK scenarios. In the first one, the teacher asks a few questions of the whole class and takes several responses from students. If this is a class of 25 students, the teacher only knows for sure that three students have some idea about the concept of reconstruction. Others may be aware, but there is no way to confirm it with the APK format used. The depth of insight in the first scenario is also limited. Though the teacher is very sincere, the effort to get all students to make connections to prior information falls short.

In the second scenario, the teacher designs the experience to engage all students, not just a few. The visual prompt elicits a wide range of responses from students. Asking students to write down words that come to mind when viewing a picture and then to discuss their list with a partner leads to many more related vocabulary words being shared—in turn forging many more connections. Both self-reflection and partner interaction are strategies that increase discussion and feedback. When the teacher gets to the question about why an era might be called "Reconstruction," she has set the stage for the students to construct the rationale, rather than telling them the definition. Finally, the follow-up question helps students realize a broader definition of reconstruction at a personal, local, and global level. Although the first APK experience would take about three minutes and the second one takes nine to ten minutes, there is no question that students' readiness to move forward is enhanced by the teacher in scenario two and is well worth the time spent.

A strong APK is open-ended, seeking to guide learners to an "aha" moment about the concept or information being taught. Consider the following brief APK interaction between teacher and students to help them grasp the idea of continental drift theory:

Teacher: I have five puzzle pieces on the ELMO. If I ask you to fit these pieces together, what are three or four things you might look for first?

Kalia: I would look at the shape of the puzzle pieces and see which parts push out and which parts are dented in.

Teacher: Can someone add to Kalia's response and tell us other thoughts that come to mind?

Shaun: I agree with Kalia. I look at the outline of the piece and where the edges go in or where they bump out and then I pick two pieces to see if they work. If they don't work, I pick up a different piece to see if I can make a match.

Teacher:	Can someone tell me what part of the puzzle piece you look at first?
Rosalinda:	Well, I look at all five pieces. I see which ones have the right shapes, and then I sort of make a picture in my head to decide which shapes might fit together.
Teacher:	Let me ask a question about today's lesson. We are talking about something called continental drift or continental movement. If you look at the Atlantic Ocean on the globe or a map, could you find anything that reminds you of a puzzle?

And the conversation continues.

ADDITIONAL STRATEGIES FOR APK

In any content area, techniques to activate prior knowledge can help make the text or other literacy resources more meaningful to students. In her book *Teaching Reading in Social Studies, Science, and Math*, author and consultant Laura Robb (2003) outlines prereading strategies that she calls getting-ready-to-learn strategies that prod thinking:

- **Brainstorm and Categorize:** Students generate a free flow of ideas and organize them under general headings. (*Think of as many words as you can that might go into a story about winter in New England.*)

- **Preview/Analyze/Connect:** Students preview aspects of the text, such as headings, graphs, pictures, and sidebars; analyze the content; and then make personal connections. The teacher models for them through think-alouds. (*How is the graph on page 82 useful to the reader? Is there a better way of communicating the information?*)

- **Fast-Write:** Students write about a topic for a few minutes to retrieve what they know. (*Write anything you can recall about George Washington.*)

- **Anticipation Guide:** The teacher creates statements about a topic to be taught and asks students to respond as to whether they think the statement is true or false.

Using APK: Discussion and Data to Assess Students' Background Knowledge

APK activities also serve as a means of assessing students' background knowledge. As such, they are suitable for students at all achievement levels and do not need to be tiered. But the information you gather from students during the activity can help you identify what students know or don't know about a topic to be taught. If the APK task in the second scenario outlined on page 39 was being used by a teacher to subsequently tier instruction, she might use the following indicators to determine how to cluster students:

Reconstruction Era: Teacher Scaffolds Tasks Based on Prior Knowledge Task

Group 1	Group 2	Group 3
• Used simple descriptive words	• Appropriately descriptive	• Used insightful words
• Limited connections to reasons it was called Reconstruction—rebuilding buildings, cities only	• Made good connections to concrete, tangible evidence, but didn't extend beyond the physically reconstructing	• Connections extended to social, emotional needs pertaining to Reconstruction
• Struggled with any connection of Reconstruction to today's world	• Had parallel ideas of reconstruction of cities in Iraq and after Hurricane Katrina	• Discussed reconstruction of families after crisis, reconstruction politically with new president—more depth to thinking

Groupings Based on Observations of Students

Marcus	Eric	Austin	Raymond	Ginny	Antonio
Clay	Kala	William	Ahmad	Anne	Jamal
Shannon		Dwayne	Deandra	Pedro	
Miguel		Beverly	Nicole	Lakeisha	
		Justine	Hannah	Danny	
		Sam	Mark		

Curriculum Content: Reconstruction Era

Essential Questions

- What measures were taken during Reconstruction to reunite a divided country? Were these actions successful?

- How did conditions in the country during the period of Reconstruction influence westward expansion?

- What changes took place in the North and South to boost economic growth following the Civil War?

- How did the rights of African Americans change in the 20 years that followed the end of the Civil War? Were these changes influenced by geography?

Terms to Know

- Reconstruction: The period following the Civil War in which Congress passed laws designed to rebuild the country and bring the southern states back into the Union

- Segregation: The separation of people, usually based on race or religion

- Discrimination: An unfair difference in the treatment of people

Problems During Reconstruction

- Millions of freed slaves needed housing, clothing, food, and jobs.

- The South's economy was in ruins.

- Money had no value.

- Banks were closed.

- Railroads, bridges, plantations, and crops were destroyed.

Measures Taken to Resolve Problems

- The Freedmen's Bureau was a government agency that provided food, schools, and medical care for freed slaves and others in the South.

- Sharecropping was a system after the war in which freedmen and poor white farmers rented land from a landowner by promising to pay the owner with a share of the crop.

- Cities grew with people, businesses, and factories.

- Railroads were a key to the expansion of business, agriculture, and industry. They facilitated the growth of small towns to cities. Railroad centers stimulated the growth of factories where clothing, furniture, and other useful items were made.

- The need for more and better roads increased.

(Adapted from the Virginia Department of Education, Social Studies Standards of Learning, 2006)

Though tiering instruction according to content will be discussed in detail in Chapter 4, below are brief examples of how content can be tiered for each group:

- **Group 1:** These students will benefit from connecting to the reconstruction efforts following the Civil War through the eyes of people involved. They will review first-person letters and accounts of life during and after the Civil War to better understand the physical, economic, social, and emotional costs associated with the war. Then, using a cause-and-effect format, students will be asked to make connections between the "costs" and efforts of Reconstruction, specifically focusing on problems during Reconstruction. A resource is http://www.eyewitnesstohistory.com/

- **Group 2:** These students have a sense of the goals of Reconstruction; however, they would benefit from understanding the complexities that come with the effort. A driving question is: *Though Lee surrendered at Appomattox, in what ways was the war still not over during the time of Reconstruction?* These students will focus on what happened to the rights of African Americans during and after Reconstruction. The following Web-based timeline of Reconstruction has resources that could be examined to respond to this question: http://chnm.gmu.edu/courses/122/recon/chron.html.

- **Group 3:** These students have strong insight into a wide range of perspectives on the role of Reconstruction, with the ability to apply their insights to what is happening in the world today and to compare current events with events following the Civil War. Their focus will be on what actions were taken to encourage economic growth during Reconstruction and determining if equivalent conditions have existed and currently exist in the United States and other parts of the world. Using the Web sites and several national and local newspapers, they will be asked to work in two groups and search out events occurring globally, nationally, and locally that compare with events during Reconstruction.

APK and the Curriculum

In considering prior knowledge, it can be helpful to examine the curriculum for earlier grade levels to take note of what previous exposure students have had to the content you will be teaching. For example, if you can say to students, "Remember when you were in third grade and you learned about the explorers Lewis and Clark?" then you can intentionally draw together past and new related content that will assist in their recall. As you examine curriculum vertically, the following questions are important to consider:

- Is this the first time students are being exposed to this content? If so, how can I find information they already know to connect to what I am about to teach?

- Is this a standard that is being spiraled throughout the grades? If so what are key terms and concepts previously taught and how can I connect with what students might have learned?

- How does this content relate to other subjects being studied at this grade level? Are there opportunities for cross-curricular connections?

Since you are prepping students for the content that will be introduced in later grades, it is also important to think about how you can help bridge to the next level. When students know that the content learned in previous years connects to what they are learning in your class and will be expanded upon as they move through the grades, they will be primed to expect or anticipate the content. Their thinking expands to become even more integrated and complex, allowing for easier retrieval of information. In addition, examination of connections across and among content areas allows you to streamline delivery of material, enabling you to cluster information into bigger ideas. The way that we activate the content students have previously learned is another important consideration in tiering: "Students need to practice, review, and drill skills, but they should do so only in the spirit of working toward more complex mastery of those skills" (Jacobs, 1997, p. 19).

Chunking the Lesson

The next step in lesson design is deciding how to chunk the lesson to fully engage students.

Specifically, we need to know how to pace and chunk lessons to accommodate learners' attention spans and their ability to stay focused on the content. A key to successful brain-compatible lesson design is to take into consideration the state of the learner. We use the term "state of the learner" because the phrase conveys the need to shift states of being or awareness in order to keep students engaged. For example, if students are sitting at a desk listening to a teacher lecture, their state is one of being a sedentary, hopefully receptive, listener. If students are in cooperative groups working on an activity, their learning state will be interactive with dialogue. When students switch from writing in a reflective learning log or journal to a partner discussion, they change learning states.

When it comes to lesson design, a rule of thumb is generally to shift students' attention states according to the age of the learner; see box at left. Frequently the shift is from one task to another, but a student's attention state can shift with activities of shorter duration, as well. Think of providing an energizing interval of two to five minutes, which can be accomplished with a content-related think-pair-share activity or simply by having students stand up and stretch. I know one sixth-grade teacher who, when she notices students getting lethargic, will have a "stop-and-chat" minute, telling students to "Stand up and tell a neighbor your favorite singer [or sport or food or what you had for breakfast]." Then she tells them, "Now that you have more oxygen in your brain, we're ready to sit

How Long Can We Keep Students' Attention?

"Teachers often wonder how long they can keep the attention of students during an instructional task. One suggested guide is to consider the student's age, then add or subtract two minutes (Jensen, 1995). Let me share how I explain to middle school teachers why sixth-grade classes are so unwieldy. Sixth graders are 12 years old. Using the age-plus-or-minus–two-minutes rule, a teacher should shift activities every 10–14 minutes. Middle school teachers have a tendency to think in terms of 20- to 25-minute instructional sections, but these are simply too long for 12-year-old learners, and that's why their lessons fall short of keeping most students engaged."

—From Teaching Smarter With the Brain in Focus (Armstrong, 2008, p. 38)

down and learn." Below is an example showing how a lesson can be chunked to change learners' states of attention.

Chunking a Lesson to Keep Students Engaged

Attention State: Student as . . .	Time	Transition During Lesson
Listener	8 minutes	The teacher uses a PowerPoint presentation to explain important content from the lesson. The students are listening to the lecture. No note taking is required.
Reflector and Note Taker	4–5 minutes	The teacher tells students to write down in their journals the key points they recall from the mini-lecture.
Collaborator	3 minutes	The teacher asks students to talk to their partners and see if they recalled similar or different information.
Summarizer Designer/Artist	7–10 minutes	The teacher combines two sets of partners for a group of four students. She gives each group a piece of chart paper and markers. She asks students to restate the information using pictures and images only.
Observer or Presenter	3 minutes	Each group gives a three-minute presentation to the class.

Keeping Students Engaged: Movement Keeps Learners on Track

A question from the survey at the end of Chapter 1 asks, "Do you design interesting and relevant lessons to hook and engage your students?" Each teacher needs to think about how to put together a lesson to maximally engage students. Once you know that the attention of the learner needs to shift focus based on the learner's age, the challenge is to make these transitions fluid, meaningful, and engaging. An engaged learner not only has more investment in the activity, but has a more active brain.

When students become physically active there is an increase of a substance known as brain-derived-neurotrophic factor, or BDNF, in the neuron. BDNF enhances the infrastructure of the cell and supports learning from three perspectives: preparing for learning, boosting recall, and increasing attention. BDNF increases in the neuron with physical activity (Ratey, 2008).

Teachers know that students thrive when they are engaged and active in the learning process, but with advances in research on the brain and learning we now know why. Lessons should not only be chunked to keep students attentive, but physical activity should be interspersed throughout a lesson. Infusing movement into a lesson can be done in the context of the lesson or simply as a break of a few minutes to change the learner's state. Each of the following examples adjusts the learner's state, but at the same time stays on topic:

- Changing from brief lecture to a small-group activity, such as moving from a review of key content in science to a carousel brain-storming activity where groups of students rotate around a room responding to review prompts on chart paper.

- Switching from journal writing to a simulation/role play in social studies on a topic such as immigration through Ellis Island.

- Transitioning from classroom-based math practice to measuring area, perimeter, and angles of the school's outdoor courtyard.

Building in breaks solely for physical activity is also purposeful. For example, students can stand behind desks and stretch, march, and/or do "fast feet" for a minute. I know one middle school Latin teacher who had students go out and walk briskly around the track before tests in his afternoon class. Several elementary teachers I know use *Brain Gym* (Dennison & Dennison, 1992) or *Smart Moves* (Hannaford, 1995) as a focus/refocus strategy. The bottom line is to remember to keep students' minds *and bodies* activated!

In addition to activating prior knowledge and changing attention states, a high-quality lesson will use instructional strategies that are well researched. In *Classroom Instruction That Works* (2001), authors Marzano, Pickering, and Pollock, leaders in applications of research-based practices to improve instruction, highlight examples of important tools that support learning.

Although each of the nine correlates of achievement they describe are important, the seven in the chart below can readily be translated to lesson design strategies.

Categories of Strategies That Affect Student Achievement

Identifying similarities and differences: Build in frequent opportunities for students to compare and contrast during a lesson.

Summarizing and note taking: Ensure that students synthesize new material in discussion and through systematic note taking, as well as learning logs and journals.

Nonlinguistic representations: Tap into visual memory systems using pictures, images, icons, and artifacts to reflect the content being taught.

Cooperative learning: Build in frequent opportunities for social interaction with both short-term partner and small-group work, as well as longer-term learning communities.

Generating and testing hypotheses: Teach students skills to identify problems and propose solutions using data and information at hand, as well as through action research.

Questions, cues, and advance organizers: Generate thinking and build connections at all times.

Setting objectives and providing feedback: Identify goals and specific "Look Fors" in guided practice and assessment that students may use to self-assess, and teachers may use in providing specific feedback to students.

Some teachers are struck by the obviousness of the need to incorporate these correlates into lesson design. "Of course, I'll ask good questions," they say, or "I use cooperative learning several times a week." But the strongest benefit is derived when teachers are intentional about every aspect of the lesson—when to direct teach, when to change learners' states, how to get students to think, how to provide meaningful feedback. If you're interested in further elaboration on these and additional correlates of achievement, see Robert Marzano's *The Art and Science of Teaching* (2007).

A Lesson Planning Template

To help you organize your thinking as you plan differentiated lessons, you may want to use the lesson planning template provided in the appendix. You'll find one with guiding questions to help you flesh out your ideas, along with an example, and a blank template.

Summary

You can develop your skill and comfort level with tiering instruction if you have a strong sense of the brain-compatible lesson components that comprise an excellent lesson as well as information about the starting points of your students. With these insights you are ready to move forward!

Ideas for Reflection

1. Select a lesson you have taught recently and analyze it to see the strengths (and weaknesses) of the lesson design. (Use the 10 Tiered Instruction Targets at the end of Chapter 1 as criteria for your review.)

2. Design a lesson in which you are introducing new content where prior knowledge is clearly developed. Assess the degree to which students seem to grasp the new content. Teach another, similar class without activating prior knowledge. Reflect on the connections that students make. Ask students to give you feedback on whether the APK activities were helpful.

3. Observe a colleague's class specifically looking at the individual's and group's ability to attend to the lesson based on the age of the learner. Look at student engagement to see if there is a relationship between shifts of attention and engagement.

4. Think about a lesson you are about to teach or one that you would like to teach. Plan for three different ways to differentiate instruction by content.

Chapter 4

Content Instruction: Tiering to Teach Essential Skills and Knowledge

"What, when, and how do I differentiate?" an obviously overwhelmed second-year teacher asked. She had sat through the faculty workshop on differentiation and approached me afterward to ask a few more questions. After a brief conversation, it was clear that what she really wanted was to be reassured that taking small steps toward differentiation was the way to get started. I assured her that her willingness to ask questions was a great first step and that moving forward a bit at a time was often a smart way to go.

What are these first small steps to tiering instruction? Because most schools and school systems have defined the curriculum content that students are expected to learn, a good place to start is by addressing the subject matter being taught. You can find this information by using some of the following support documents that are likely available to you:

- Pacing guide—a framework of the content standards or objectives and the order and time frame in which they are expected to be taught.

- Curriculum guide—an overview of information and skills to be taught in a given subject area with specific emphasis on facts and concepts that must be covered because they will be *on the test*.

- Scope and sequence—similar to a pacing guide, this document is typically included with all commercially published textbooks and provides information about how the text is organized, including the order in which content is presented (sequence) and the breadth (scope) of coverage.

If you are tentative about teaching the prescribed curriculum because you think the learning targets aren't appropriate for some students, ask yourself, "Is the designated content too difficult or is it the way I intend to teach it that might cause some learners to be left behind?" Most of the time it is not the content itself that makes the learning targets unattainable; rather, it is the degree to which the subject matter is undifferentiated and the effectiveness of strategies selected to teach the targeted goals. Carol Tomlinson and Jay McTighe (2006) remind us that "desired understandings and questions should remain a constant target, regardless of differences in students' background knowledge, interests, and preferred learning modalities" (p. 33).

Knowing the *What* of the Lesson

Like peeling back the layers of an onion, unpacking state standards or instructional learning objectives can reveal various levels of information. Here are four helpful questions to ask when examining a content standard from the curriculum or pacing guide:

- What thinking processes are involved? (Check the verbs: *analyze, compare and contrast, investigate, demonstrate*, and so on.)

- What key vocabulary must be learned?

- How do the conjunctions *and* and *or* in the standard influence what a student must know and be able to do? Thorough reading of standards will tell if there are several steps or methods of understanding that students must demonstrate.

- What kind of support can a student access? For example, can a calculator be used? Will Internet or primary resources be accessible?

The math example below illustrates how a standard can be unpacked for greater clarity.

After examining the verbs in the standard above, a fifth-grade math teacher knows that students are being asked to *analyze* and *express*. Analysis includes knowing how the structure of numerical and geometric patterns changes or

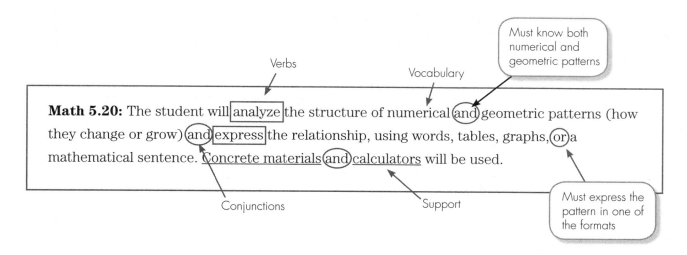

grows. Students can show (express) their knowledge using words, tables, graphs, or a mathematical sentence. Typically, when options for demonstrating knowledge are provided (as in the example above, where students can use "words, tables, graphs, or a mathematical sentence"), it means that the end-of-grade or end-of-course test may have questions using any of the methods of expression. It is advisable for a teacher to address all concepts where the conjunction is "or" because any portion of the learning goal may be tested. You should analyze all standards or learning objectives in this manner to ensure that your lessons allow students to interact with content in the manner in which it will be assessed. Please note that I did not say "Teach to the test." The point is to be smart about communicating the language of a given standard so that students know what they might encounter on a test. The Teacher Self-Checklist for Tiering Lessons on page 54 will guide you as you think about differentiating instruction with a specific learning standard or objective in mind.

A Tiered Instruction Imperative: Choosing Content Based on Instructional Reading Levels

If students have a diet only of books that are too difficult, reading competence actually decreases (Routman, 2003). Students get frustrated at repeatedly missing words and give up trying, or students run through the text missing

Teacher Self-Checklist for Tiering Lessons Based on Content

Questions to Consider	Notes
1. What is the content that I am to teach for this lesson or unit?	
2. What does the learning target tell me that students need to know and be able to do?	
3. Which information is most essential to the learner?	
4. What are the big ideas of this lesson or unit?	
5. What does the verb tell me about the level of thinking that this standard requires?	
6. What are the conjunctions? Will I need to have students demonstrate knowledge in multiple ways?	
7. What are the key vocabulary terms that students must learn?	
8. Are the vocabulary terms part of each student's existing background knowledge or will I need to build this understanding for all or a portion of the class?	
9. If a portion, which students will need to have additional support to acquire content vocabulary?	
10. How will I determine what my students already know so I can build upon and scaffold their learning?	
11. How can I make sure that students connect the big ideas to their world?	
12. Can related content be brought in to expand thinking and provide enrichment for students who move ahead quickly?	

Additional Questions:

A Practical Guide to Tiering Instruction in the Differentiated Classroom © 2010 by Sarah Armstrong, Scholastic Professional

essential vocabulary, with markedly reduced comprehension. At the same time, reading lots of easy books is not enough for continued growth because when students read only at their independent levels, scaffolding up to the next level of performance does not occur. For these reasons, as discussed in Chapter 2, matching the reader with an appropriate text is essential, since true learning occurs when the task difficulty and skill level required are slightly above the student's level.

Matching students with texts at their instructional levels seems to be conventional practice in language arts in the early grades. Around fourth grade, leveled reading groups in language arts become less frequent, often replaced by whole-class literature selections. By middle school, reading at instructional levels is seen as embarrassing to students who are reading below level, and so the practice is abandoned—abandoning also the hope for many students to move forward. The bottom line is that students need multiple and sustained opportunities to read literature and text at their instructional reading level. This need exists in both English/language arts classes and in content classes. One way to support students in content classes is to give them access to nonfiction leveled readers.

Criteria for leveled readers are based on an analysis of published books that have been officially leveled using the Fountas & Pinnell Reading Recovery and Lexile leveling criteria, as well as other factors known to affect text difficulty. An extensive list of criteria and book attributes has been developed for each level. This list is an excellent resource when planning for tiered lessons by content.

A few years ago, I worked with a middle school principal to figure out a way to find the instructional reading levels for his 200 entering students. Though he received recommendations from fifth-grade teachers from four elementary schools, he wanted to verify the levels while at the same time build greater insight on the part of his sixth-grade teachers on using instructional reading levels to differentiate instruction.

Different assessment tools were employed, according to the reading levels of students. To ensure reliability of the assessment, we arranged for reading specialists and instructional coaches from the elementary schools to come to the middle school for three days in October to administer an Informal Reading Inventory (IRI) to any sixth grader reading at fourth-grade level or below. The remaining students took the Star Reading Inventory.

Text Gradient Guide

Type of Reader	Fountas & Pinnell Level	Lexile Level	Basal Level	Grade Level
Emergent	A		Readiness	Kindergarten/Grade 1
	B		Pre-primer 1	Kindergarten/Grade 1
Early	C		Pre-primer 1	Kindergarten/Grade 1
	D		Pre-primer 2	Grade 1
	E	200–400 L	Pre-primer 3	Grade 1
	F		Primer	Grade 1
	G			Grade 1
Transitional	H		Grade 1	Grades 1/2
	I			Grades 1/2
	J	140–500 L	Grade 2	Grade 2
	K			Grade 2
	L			Grades 2/3
	M	330–700 L		Grades 2/3
Self-Extending	N		Grade 3	Grade 3
	O			Grades 3/4
	P	445–810 L		Grades 3/4
	Q		Grade 4	Grade 4
	R			Grade 4
Advanced	S			Grades 4/5
	T	565–910 L		Grades 4/5
	U		Grade 5	Grade 5
	V			Grades 5/6
	W	665–1000 L		Grades 5/6
	X		Grade 6	Grades 6/7/8
	Y	735–1065 L	Grade 7	Grades 6/7/8
	Z	805–1100 L	Grade 8/beyond	Grades 7/8

Adapted from Fountas, I., & Pinnell, G. (2006). Leveled Books (K–8): Matching Texts to Readers for Effective Teaching. Portsmouth, NH: Heinemann. http://www.lexile.com

These assessments were real eye-openers for teachers, who found that approximately four out of ten students were reading below grade level. As a result, key English teachers became staunch advocates for placing students in books at appropriate reading levels. In fact, after forming a new goal that all students are expected to become readers of a wide range of books and other materials, the dedicated reading lists were discarded! Instead of the whole class plodding through a single book that the teacher and students read aloud together, self-selected books became the norm, with teachers homing in on strategies by selecting passages from a wide range of books. A single book might be selected for shared reading to increase vocabulary and build listening comprehension, but *students as readers* became a way of life in English classes overall.

Using Supplemental Nonfiction Books to Tier Content Instruction

In this middle school, the responsibility for placing students in texts at their instructional reading levels rested not only with the English teachers. Armed with information about reading levels and the knowledge that the readabilities of most textbooks are above the level of intended use, teachers in core subject areas also became acutely aware of the challenge that nearly four out of ten students faced when they were asked to read the textbook. Teachers resolved to add supplemental nonfiction resources to a literacy library at the middle school. These books did not sit on an individual teacher's shelf; rather, they were housed as book sets in a room off the library accessible to all teachers.

Expanding Beyond the Textbook

Leveled supplemental books that support the established curricula afford teachers the ability to tier content lessons by reading levels. A number of publishers, such as Newbridge, Benchmark, Scholastic, and National Geographic, cluster books by topics at a variety of reading levels and make

Books by Genre at a Range of Reading Levels

(Fountas & Pinnell Guided Reading levels shown)

The following examples show that all students can be engaged in a genre or book study using books that have been appropriately matched with instructional reading levels. In these examples, the content has been differentiated or tiered by reading level, but the main concept or understanding remains the same for all students. Keep in mind that student interest should also be considered when matching students to texts. Students with an extensive interest in a topic will likely be able to tackle a text at a higher reading level because of enriched background knowledge or deep attraction to the subject matter.

Realistic Fiction (Humorous)

- *Horrible Harry* by Suzy Kline (level L)
- *Freckle Juice* by Judy Blume (level M)
- *Ramona Quimby* by Beverly Cleary (level O)
- *Beetles, Lightly Toasted* by Phyllis Reynolds Naylor (Level Q)
- *In the Year of the Boar and Jackie Robinson* by Bette Bao Lord (level R)
- *Maniac Magee* by Jerry Spinelli (level W)

Realistic Fiction (Adventurous)

- *Stone Fox* by John Reynolds Gardiner (level P)
- *Hatchet* by Gary Paulsen (level R)
- *Bridge to Terabithia* by Katherine Paterson (level T)

Mystery

- *Cam Jansen* by David A. Adler (level L)
- *Boxcar Children: Mystery in Washington, D.C.* by Gertrude Chandler Warner (level O)
- *Encyclopedia Brown* by Donald J. Sobol (level P)
- *Mystery of the Cupboard* by Lynne Reid Banks (level R)
- *The Westing Game* by Ellen Raskin (level V)

Fantasy

- *James and the Giant Peach* by Roald Dahl (level Q)
- *Charlotte's Web* by E.B. White (level R)
- *Poppy* by Avi (level S)
- *The Lion, the Witch, and the Wardrobe* by C.S. Lewis (level T)
- *Tale of Despereaux* by Kate DiCamillo (level U)
- *Harry Potter* by J.K. Rowling (level V)
- *Wrinkle in Time* by Madeleine L'Engle (level W)
- *Redwall* by Brian Jacques (level Z)

Author Study – Jean Craighead George

- *There's an Owl in the Shower* by Jean Craighead George (level Q)
- *Cry of the Crow* by Jean Craighead George (level S)
- *My Side of the Mountain* by Jean Craighead George (level U)

Biographical Study – Pocahontas

- *The True Story of Pocahontas* by Dr. Linwood "Little Bear" Custalow and Angela L. Daniel "Silver Star" (level L)
- *Pocahontas and the Strangers* by Clyde Robert Bulla (level N)
- *In Their Own Words: Pocahontas* by George Sullivan (level R)

Web Sites for Book Leveling Information

http://registration.beavton.k12.or.us/lbdb/default.htm

http://src.scholastic.com/ecatalog/

these materials available in sets. In some cases, the cover of the text and the visual representations appear the same, but the readability varies. These books are typically content-rich while at the same time tailored for readability. Although some publishers have graduated sets of leveled nonfiction books on specific topics, many times a teacher will need to search out the content from a variety of sources.

A common question teachers have when they differentiate by instructional reading levels is, "How do I incorporate leveled books without making my struggling readers feel self-conscious?" A particular concern is ensuring that students don't feel as if they are in—as they call it—"the baby books."

I watched a middle school physical science teacher do an exceptional job in a lesson on magnetism that incorporated leveled readers in stations around the room. Her strategy was to have a range of nonfiction leveled readers at each station. Her students were in mixed groups, but each student had an assignment card. At one point, the highest-achieving students were asked to compare a particularly well-done visual organizer in a nonfiction book at a lower readability level with one in a high school text. The task was to analyze the two graphics to see if the content was effectively represented in both. In contrast, her lowest-achieving students were asked to look at a picture in the on-level text and to respond to specific questions based on the picture. In effect, all students looked at a range of materials. However, when it came to completing the study guide, the teacher manipulated the actual reading and response by placing students in materials at their instructional reading levels.

Do students figure out that some of them are in different books at different levels? Certainly, but you can orchestrate the use of materials in such a way that students realize that all resources can support learning. A first step is to create a culture of respect for the different entry points of learners and make it clear that using a wide variety of resources at a range of levels is the norm. Designing lessons so that all students use leveled materials is important, as well. A student at a higher reading level might use a nonfiction supplemental text at a lower level with a question or task that has greater complexity. If you think about it, you may have enjoyed reading nonfiction text with your own children at home and found that you learned something new or interesting. In this case, the art of developing the questions or tasks come into play.

Examples of Supplemental Books on a Specific Topic or Standard

3rd Grade: Topic—Civics: The student will recognize why government is necessary in the classroom, school, and community. The student will explain the importance of the basic principles that form the foundation of a republican form of government.

Title/Author	Publisher	Fountas & Pinnell Level
Following Rules, by Robin Nelson	Lerner	Level I
We Vote, by Cynthia Martin	Newbridge	Level K
What Is Democracy?, by Julie Haydon	Harcourt	Level N
If You Were There When They Signed the Constitution, by Elizabeth Levy	Scholastic	Level P
Making a Law, by Sarah DeCapra	Scholastic	Level P

4th Grade: Topic—Weather: The student will investigate and understand how weather conditions and phenomena occur and can be predicted. Key concepts include weather measurements and meteorological tools (air pressure: barometer; wind speed: anemometer; rainfall: rain gauge; and temperature: thermometer) and weather phenomena (fronts, clouds, and storms).

Title/Author	Publisher	Fountas & Pinnell Level
Looking at Clouds, by S. Ring	Newbridge	Level L
Stormy Weather, by N. Lunis	Benchmark	Level N
Weather Words, by Gail Gibbons	Scholastic	Level R
And Now for the Weather!, by W. O'Byrne	Rigby	Level S/T

A Practical Guide to Tiering Instruction in the Differentiated Classroom © 2010 by Sarah Armstrong, Scholastic Professional

5th Grade: Topic—Matter: The student will investigate and understand that matter is anything that has mass, takes up space, and occurs as a solid, liquid, or gas.

Title/Author	Publisher	Fountas & Pinnell Level
What Is Matter?, by Lisa Trumbauer	Newbridge	Level J
My World of Science: Solids, Liquids, Gases, by Angela Royston	Heinemann	Level L
Ranger Rick: The World of Matter, by Ron Cole	Newbridge	Level N
Properties of Matter: Blue Planet Diaries, by Lisa Boehm	Newbridge	Level S
Science Concepts: Matter, by Alvin Silverstein, Virginia Silverstein, and Laura S. Nunn	Lerner	Level Y

6th Grade: Topic—American Revolution: The student will demonstrate knowledge of the causes and results of the American Revolution by identifying the issues of dissatisfaction that led to the American Revolution and identifying how political ideas shaped the revolutionary movement.

Title/Author	Publisher	Fountas & Pinnell Level
Sam the Minuteman, by Nathaniel Benchley	HarperTrophy	Level J
Revolutionary War on Wednesday, by Mary Pope Osbourne	Random House	Level M
Redcoats and Petticoats, by Katherine Kirkpatrick	Hampton-Brown	Level P
If You Lived at the Time of the American Revolution, by Kay Moore	Scholastic	Level Q
A Time Line of the American Revolution, by Lynn George	Rosen	Level R
The Start of the American Revolutionary War: Paul Revere Rides at Midnight, by Allison S. Draper	Rosen	Level S
The American Revolution, by Bruce Bliven, Jr.	Random House	Level T
George vs. George: The American Revolution as Seen From Both Sides, by Rosalyn Schanzer	National Geographic	Level U
Fight for Freedom: The American Revolutionary War, by Benson Bobrick	Scholastic	Level X

Rewriting to Adapt Texts

As we've discussed, to successfully differentiate using tiered content you must know the reading levels of your students and have resources at both their independent and instructional levels. If commercial resources are not available, you can adapt text yourself to be sure all students have access to the targeted facts and concepts of the lesson. Certainly, the thought of rewriting text to teach students the content of the class can be a bit daunting, but finding the key content and being selective about which text is rewritten can make it more manageable.

Let's look at an example. In Pennsylvania, the Northwest Ordinance is mentioned as a primary document that is taught to sixth-grade students to illustrate how the early government solved conflict through compromise. This 1787 document addresses questions of state expansion and designates

Teacher resource of literacy library book bins of nonfiction topics

Literacy Library housing Leveled Reading Books for teachers

slave or free states. (The ordinance text can be found at http://www.teachingamericanhistory.org/library/index.asp?document=48.) Consider the original and clarified versions of portions of Articles 5 and 6 shown below.

Take note that the rewritten version takes into account historical context in that free inhabitants in 1787 did not include women.

The Northwest Ordinance, Articles 5 and 6

original	adapted and clarified version
Article 5 excerpt: And, whenever any of the said States shall have sixty thousand free inhabitants therein, such State shall be admitted, by its delegates, into the Congress of the United States, on an equal footing with the original States in all respects whatever, and shall be at liberty to form a permanent constitution and State government: Provided, the constitution and government so to be formed, shall be republican, and in conformity to the principles contained in these articles.	*Article 5 excerpt adapted:* When a new state has 60,000 free men (women do not count), its delegates will be admitted into Congress on an equal footing with delegates from the original 13 states. The new state can form its own permanent constitution and state government as long as the state constitution conforms to the principles stated in the Northwest Ordinance.
Article 6: There shall be neither slavery nor involuntary servitude in the said territory, otherwise than in the punishment of crimes whereof the party shall have been duly convicted: Provided, always, that any person escaping into the same, from whom labor or service is lawfully claimed in any one of the original States, such fugitive may be lawfully reclaimed and conveyed to the person claiming his or her labor or service as aforesaid.	*Article 6 adapted:* Slavery or forcing someone to work against his or her will is not allowed, unless someone has been lawfully convicted and it is part of the punishment for the crime. But if a person escapes from slavery or from being a servant in one of the original states, he or she is considered a fugitive and can be reclaimed and sent back to the person for whom he or she worked.

Tiering Vocabulary

As you prepare to tier content, you should also be aware of the ease or difficulty of the related vocabulary. Since we know that increasing student exposure to new terms is one way to enrich thinking, vocabulary instruction that builds on the APK experience by connecting new words to what students already know can be highly beneficial. In fact, Robert Marzano points out that "instruction in words that are specific to the content being taught is associated with a gain of 33 percentile points" (2004, p. 89).

Tiering vocabulary instruction is illustrated in the following content related to plate tectonics and the creation of geologic features—a familiar upper elementary and middle school science standard. These science terms are commonly found in science texts and curriculum guides that address the topic of plate tectonics. Because you want to begin with the end in mind and be aware of key vocabulary on end-of-grade, end-of-course, unit, or end-of-chapter tests, you should be able to take vocabulary related to the content you will be teaching and rank it according to how essential it is to the material overall. The following groupings start with basic vocabulary related to plate tectonics and include vocabulary that will be on the test in one form or another. The second group is called basic plus, which includes the essential terms from the

Vocabulary Group 1 (Basic— terms will be on the test)	Vocabulary Group 2 (Basic plus)	Vocabulary Group 3 (Expanded)
fault	crustal plate movement	geophysical processes
fold	continental drift	trenches—names and locations of
ridge	fissure volcanoes	collision zones
volcano	strike-slip faults	subduction zones
magma	geological features	geologic map reading
earthquake		
plate tectonics		

first group and additional standard vocabulary. The final group expands on the vocabulary in the first and second groups, adding geologic map–reading terms and additional related language. The third group is an example of providing expanded vocabulary to students who will benefit from enrichment tasks related to the content

After identifying the targeted vocabulary for each level, the next step in lesson design is to determine strategies to teach these terms most effectively. All students should be taught the essential vocabulary that they will encounter on the test; however, in a tiered lesson, additional or related terminology can be taught to students who quickly master the essential vocabulary. Additionally, knowing the vocabulary from prior standards can help you work with students who may not have previously mastered this content, so meeting with the previous grade's teachers to discuss vertical alignment of vocabulary is a good idea.

Tier the Assessment Too!

Remember that you need to adjust assessment when you tier content. Consider the vocabulary words related to plate tectonics and geologic features. When testing students who have learned only the basic terminology, you would not ask questions about the expanded vocabulary and concepts. Regardless of the format of assessment, tests need to be modified so that students are held accountable only for the content they have been taught.

Summary

The following steps should be considered in tiering content:

1. Identify the standard (with attention on the verb, vocabulary, and support available). The content standard remains the same for all of our learners.

2. Determine the big idea of the standard. This essential understanding remains the same for all of our learners.

3. Pre-assess to determine students' readiness levels, interests, or learning profiles. (See Chapters 2 and 6 for pre-assessment ideas.)

4. Know the reading levels of your students and ensure access to an array of content resources at different reading levels.

5. Activate prior knowledge as a way to prime the brain and to hook students into the lesson.

6. Design engaging activities rooted in best practices for on-grade-level students. Design similar activities for struggling learners with additional support, materials, and/or instruction, and more-complex activities for advanced learners.

7. Monitor and adjust as students participate in the instructional activities.

Ideas for Reflection

1. Select a content lesson you are about to teach. Use the Teacher Self-Checklist on page 55 and reflect on what you could do to tier the lesson to a greater extent.

2. Talk to teachers at your grade level or in your learning community. Discuss the need for leveled texts and/or readers in your grade, content area, or school. Are resources available to enable you to provide materials at different levels, but with similar content?

3. Take a particularly challenging area of content that your students are required to know for the standards test. Rewrite all or a portion of the content so it can be understood more readily. Discuss with colleagues the possibility of developing a "library" of materials that can be made available to teachers.

4. Select a content area where vocabulary is an emphasis. Level the vocabulary into three or four groups. Decide on strategies that could be used effectively to support students in learning the vocabulary.

Chapter 5

Process: Strategic Teaching to Tier Instruction

Have you ever played a familiar tune on an electric piano? Even if you haven't progressed beyond the one-finger technique, at a push of a button you can add a trumpet or flute tone to the piece of music. All you have to do is press another switch to infuse the rhythms of rock and roll, a Latin beat, or rap. Tiering instruction based on *processes* of teaching is similar. The basic notes are the same, but the complexity of the music is intentionally adjusted for different learners.

Tiering by process—the *how* of teaching—is an essential consideration for meeting the needs of diverse learners in your classroom. After you've analyzed the content you teach, the next step is to differentiate through whole-group instruction, in small groups, or with individual support. You also determine the best techniques to use to support learning. Consider the questions on page 68, which prompt thinking about this aspect of differentiation, and examine one middle-school content-area teacher's notes on how she'll tier her lesson. A blank template is on page 140 in the appendix.

The art of effectively tiering instruction begins with assessing where students are and analyzing where they should go next, then selecting the most effective way of teaching each student to meet the learning targets. This decision about how to teach, referred to as instructional *pedagogy*, is defined by one group of prominent researchers as "assisting students through interaction and activity in the ongoing academic and social events of the classroom" (Tharp, 2002). In this explanation of pedagogy, teachers must guide learning while actively engaging students—now *that's* what we're about!

12 Questions to Prompt Decisions About Tiering by Process

How Will I Engage Students?	Notes
1. What information about my students have I learned from the pre-assessments?	Look at the readiness scaffold summary.
2. What grouping arrangements are optimal at different stages of the lesson? (When do I use whole-group, small-group, partner, or individual tasks?)	8 min. whole group 5 min. individual 12 min. small group Back to whole group
3. What leveled books and resources do I have to support learning? Do I need to secure additional materials?	Newbridge readers, text, Internet
4. What strategies will I use to make connections to what students know already (activate prior knowledge)?	A to Z review and inspiration webbing
5. What degree of choice should I offer to students at each tier?	TBD
6. What are entry levels of thinking for students at each tier?	Readiness scale and Independent Reading Inventories
7. What questions can I pose to scaffold or extend thinking?	Need to develop
8. How much complexity in a task or assignment can students, pairs, or groups manage?	Look at the readiness scaffold summary.
9. How quickly or how slowly should tasks advance for each tier of students?	Keep track of Group 1 to be sure they move along.
10. How much independence will specific students, pairs, or groups be able to handle and how much support will I need to provide?	Group 3 will work in library for last 15 minutes.
11. What will be the most effective strategies to use to deliver content?	Group 2 is larger. Will use jigsaw technique.
12. How will I measure student progress?	Re-administer pre-assessment

A Practical Guide to Tiering Instruction in the Differentiated Classroom © 2010 by Sarah Armstrong, Scholastic Professional

In Chapter 2, we discussed the Student Scaffolding Readiness Scale, which can help you identify specific students' readiness for learning (see page 138). Gaining increased awareness of the strengths and weaknesses of students allows you to more effectively group students for instruction. When preparing to differentiate strategies for teaching, critical areas to consider are students' background knowledge, complexity of thinking, the degree of independence they can handle, and the amount of time allotted for learning. As indicated on the chart on page 70, the teacher's role is one of providing the optimal support for each student. As you answer the questions about the needs of your students and identify how they are progressing, you can then move to the next step by selecting strategies that encourage maximum engagement.

When differentiating by process, it is not necessary to do three entire lessons from scratch. You will become more adept at developing a core lesson and adapting it based on your student groups and their areas of need. I offer several examples on the following pages. Keep in mind as well that there is a place for whole-group instruction, particularly for the following purposes:

- To provide an overview of a lesson through a mini-lecture that sets the stage for the tiered instruction to follow.

- To use resources such as a video clips, modeled lessons, guest presenters, or online sources that address the content and are suitable for all levels.

- To conduct a task or assignment that is the same, yet differentiated in the sense that students work on the same task at their own levels. Examples of these tasks might be having all students complete a compare-and-contrast graphic organizer on a given topic, do a quick-write, or complete an interactive notebook entry.

Differentiating by Process: Teacher Role

Descriptor	For students below level, teacher	For students on level, teacher	For students above level, teacher
Background Knowledge	• Provides targeted instruction • Makes connections with student interests • Builds background before story • Reinforces meaning kinesthetically • Pinpoints essential vocabulary • Uses word walls or vocabulary posters with words and icons • Provides audio or video support	• Activates and develops background information and new information • Makes connections with student interests • Expands vocabulary with connected terms/definitions	• Applies background knowledge to new information in ways that show interconnectedness of concepts • Promotes study of advanced vocabulary and higher expectations for work
Thinking	• Introduces one concept at a time • Guides students to make connections from known to new content • Creates bridges to help students move from low to high levels • Activates visual memory systems to support thinking • Uses divergent questions to build fluency, flexibility, and confidence in thinking	• Provides instruction that encourages and fosters independent thinking • Designs questions and activities to activate higher-order thinking • Uses visual memory systems to support thinking • Uses divergent questions to extend fluency, flexibility, and confidence in thinking	• Provides students with an advanced level of challenge • Facilitates opportunities for students to frame, analyze, and synthesize information to solve problems and answer questions • Provides opportunities for divergent and creative thinking in context • Solicits elaboration, innovation, and originality in thinking
Independence	• Provides clear expectations • Models and thinks aloud with students • Provides multiple opportunities for practice • Examines proximity of seating • Alters groupings, as needed • Incorporates use of mentors and tutors	• Provides choice for students • Incorporates goal-setting for all students • Provides teacher support that advances student independence • Incorporates conferencing with all students	• Provides choices of tasks or modes of learning • Incorporates learning contracts to personalize content • Encourages independent study
Time for Learning	• Provides extended time • Breaks assignments into shorter segments or "chunks"	• Provides age-appropriate pace of instruction	• Compacts curriculum or exempts students from work in which they show mastery

Tiering a Lesson: Common Goals Using Different Strategies

When planning tiered instruction, find the similarities in what students need to learn and do, then adapt lessons for each group. These guidelines apply to each grouping:

- The same learning goal is applied.
- The format of the activity remains the same.
- Tasks are engaging, challenging, and respectful.
- Groups show increasing complexity of thinking in a particular domain.

The example tiered activity below on electricity (typically in a fourth- or fifth-grade curriculum) has a common learning goal that requires students to investigate and understand the characteristics of electricity, including the key concepts of conductors and insulators and basic circuits, as well as open/closed and parallel/series circuits. The format of the lesson is similar in that students are working in small groups and recording information on a graphic organizer. Tasks for each group are interesting and engaging, although student task cards or response sheets vary according to the group. Group 1 has a slightly less complex task than Group 2 and Group 3 is somewhat more complex. Different graphic organizers are used to record work as noted in the examples on pages 73 and 74.

Tiering a Science Lesson Topic: Electricity

Group 1 (Below Level)	Group 2 (At Level)	Group 3 (Above Level)
How can we get a light bulb to light in two different ways, using one light bulb, two wires, and two batteries? Use materials to create a parallel and series circuit. After you have created your circuits, use the word cards to label the different examples. Then, sort the word and picture cards provided as either parallel or series examples. There are blank cards on which you can create and test your own examples. When is the bulb brighter—series or parallel?	What are multiple ways that we can get a light bulb to light, using several light bulbs, wires, and batteries? Create examples of parallel and series circuits. Create a label for each of the types of circuits. Then, create a chart showing which circuits work, which do not work, and why. Be sure to add an additional battery, wire, light, etc. to your trials to test your hypothesis. When is the bulb brighter—series or parallel?	What is the relationship of resistance, voltage, and current in series and parallel circuits? Create and view multiple examples of parallel and series circuits. Create a matrix to show the level of bulb brightness in each. Use the terms *resistance*, *voltage*, and *current* to describe what is causing the differences in brightness. You've just discovered Ohm's law!

Entry Points

A student's entry point is his or her readiness level. This term refers to the point at which a student can successfully engage with the content. As with instructional reading levels, entry points are above independent level and below frustration level. Before determining entry points, take that first step to examine the content and identify a progression of skills from prerequisite to more advanced understandings. Based on a range of formal and informal pre-assessments, you would first identify where students should be placed on the continuum. Some curriculum materials are developed with added suggestions for students who need support and those who need enrichment. These supplemental resources will often have suggestions for you as you plan for tiered instruction.

A Practical Guide to Tiering Instruction in the Differentiated Classroom © 2010 by Sarah Armstrong, Scholastic Professional

Group 1 example

Name _Scott_

Which bulb is brighter – Parallel or Series Circuit?

Directions: How can we get a light bulb to light in at least two different ways? Use the batteries, battery holders, wires, lamps, alligator clips and lamp holders to create a parallel and series circuit. Then, sort the word and picture cards provided as either parallel or series examples. There are blank cards where you can add other observations or illustrations. When is the bulb brighter – series or parallel?

Parallel Circuit	Series Circuit
When one bulb or battery is broken, the remaining bulbs or batteries **continue to work.**	When one bulb or battery is broken, the **entire circ** working.
There is **more than one path** for current to flow.	There is **one path** for flow.
More wires	Less Wire

Conclusion: Which bulb is brighter?

2 batteries, 1 bulb: ☐ Parallel ☒ Series ☐ Same level of brightness

1 battery, 2 bulbs: ☒ Parallel ☐ Series ☐ Same level of brightness

Group 2 example

Name _Julie_

Which bulb is brighter – Parallel or Series Circuit?

Directions: What are multiple ways that we can get a light bulb to light, using several light bulbs, wires, and batteries? Create examples of parallel and series circuits. Create a label for each of the types of circuits. Then, create a chart showing what circuits work, do not work, and why. Be sure to add an additional battery, wire, light, etc. to your trials to test your hypothesis. When is the bulb brighter – series or parallel?

Parallel Circuit	Series Circuit	Neither
Why: The wires are connected to metal that conducts electricity and makes lots of paths.	**Why:** The electricity keeps flowing along the wires in one big circle.	**Why:** The wire has to touch metal to work.

Conclusion: Which bulb is brighter? The parallel circuit is brighter when you add more bulbs. The series circuit is brighter when you add more batteries.

Group 3 example

Name **BILL**

Which bulb is brighter – Parallel or Series Circuit?

Directions: How are parallel and series circuits related to bulb brightness? Create and draw multiple examples of parallel and series circuits. Examine the resistance, voltage, and current of each circuit by recording on the matrix. Then, mark overall which circuits were had the brightest bulbs, with 1 being the brightest and 6 being the least bright. What conclusions can you make about bulb brightness?

PARALLEL CIRCUITS			
Diagram	Resistance (# bulbs)	Voltage (#batteries)	Current (Brightness)
	2	1	3
	3	1	4
	1	2	2

SERIES CIRCUITS			
Diagram	Resistance (#bulbs)	Voltage (#batteries)	Current (Brightness)
	2	1	5
	3	1	6
	1	2	1

Conclusions: Batteries in series increase voltage and make the bulbs brighter. Batteries in parallel do not seem to change the brightness. They appear to be the same as with one battery. Bulbs in series make the bulbs the least bright. Bulbs in parallel do not seem to decrease in brightness much. This may be because there are multiple paths to get voltage to the bulbs in a parallel circuit instead of one path (more resistance) in a series circuit.

The great thing about tiering is that you can always adjust! If the entry point proves too easy, move the student forward. If the entry point is too challenging, adjust the student's level downward.

To help explain entry points more completely, consider a math concept that you are trying to teach, for example, division. What are the foundational understandings that you want all students to know? Most likely, you want all students to begin by understanding what it means to divide. What is the concept of division? Once students have this understanding, there are varying levels of difficulty within division. For example, if a student had just learned the concept of division, you certainly wouldn't have them next divide multiple-digit numbers with remainders. Instead, you'd follow a continuum that allowed skills to be naturally scaffolded based on students' readiness; see example continuum for division, below. This is where pre-assessments are so beneficial. If you have identified specific skills that students should master and have placed them on a learning continuum, pre-assessments can help you identify what students already understand and what is an appropriate entry point. Based on pre-assessments of students' skill with division, this classroom teacher determined that students are at three different entry points. Some students are ready for multiple-digit by multiple-digit division. Others are ready for the more complex concept of relating fractions and division; however, because this is a new progression, the teacher would begin developing this relationship by using "friendly" fractions to help make the connections more visible. The remaining students have some understanding of the relationship of fractions and decimals and are ready for problems including some "unfriendly" fractions.

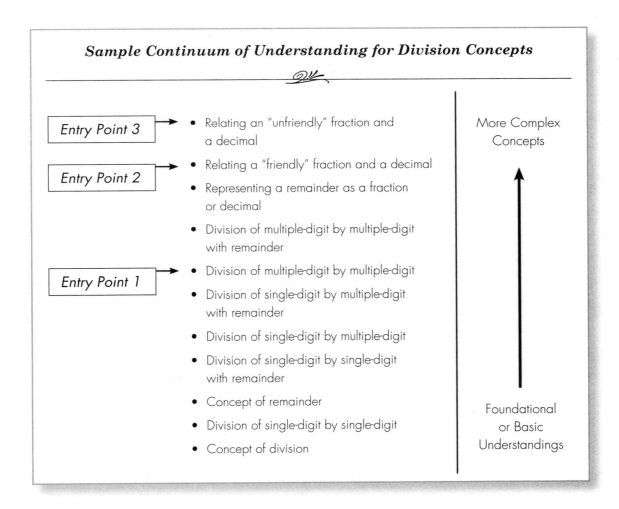

Sample Continuum of Understanding for Division Concepts

Entry Point 3
- Relating an "unfriendly" fraction and a decimal

More Complex Concepts

Entry Point 2
- Relating a "friendly" fraction and a decimal
- Representing a remainder as a fraction or decimal
- Division of multiple-digit by multiple-digit with remainder

Entry Point 1
- Division of multiple-digit by multiple-digit
- Division of single-digit by multiple-digit with remainder
- Division of single-digit by multiple-digit
- Division of single-digit by single-digit with remainder
- Concept of remainder
- Division of single-digit by single-digit
- Concept of division

Foundational or Basic Understandings

Now, consider the problems that were given to a fifth-grade math class, based on the varying entry points identified. What do the problems have in common? How does the complexity vary? The problems have been intentionally selected to meet the same learning goal of understanding division but at these varying entry points.

Entry Point 1	Entry Point 2	Entry Point 3
I want to walk long enough to burn calories from eating ice cream (225 calories). Walking burns 25 calories every 10 minutes. How many minutes do I need to walk?	I want to ride my bike long enough to burn calories from eating potato chips (150 calories). Biking burns 40 calories every 10 minutes. How many minutes do I need to ride my bike?	I want to run long enough to burn calories from eating chocolate cookies (55 calories). Running burns 80 calories every 10 minutes. How many minutes do I need to run?
Task	Task	Task
Division with no remainders (Answer: 90 minutes)	Division with "friendly" fractions (Answer: 37 ½ minutes)	Division with "unfriendly" fractions (Answer: 6 ⅞ minutes)

Adapted from Alcaru, Alston & Katims (2000)

In the example above, notice that the figures have changed, but the overall learning goal is the same for all students—understanding the relationship between fractions and division. However, the questions increase in mathematical complexity, with the first example using numbers that are easily divisible, the second example using numbers that involve "friendly" fractional increments, and the third example using numbers that involve "unfriendly" fractional increments. Adjusting tiers based on the complexity of thinking asked of students requires that you think critically about the content as well. Ask yourself: What are the prerequisite understandings? What are the more advanced understandings? Is there a hierarchy to follow in which one understanding builds upon another?

As another example, let's consider fourth grader Alexandra's level of readiness when it comes to the reading strategy of making inferences. The goal is for Alexandra to be able to grasp word meaning, understand characters' emotions, and make predictions based on inferences from the text. Although the teacher has been working with Alexandra to help her interact more with the text, she knows that Alexandra will need extra support in making inferences. In addition, she will need many opportunities for practice, which must be kept in mind when pacing instruction. Since Alexandra follows moderately complex instructions and wants more autonomy in learning, offering choice and allowing open-ended responses are important ingredients of her instruction.

As the teacher plans, she creates balanced instructional learning goals for this student. For example, if Alexandra is "low" in background knowledge on the content about which she'll be asked to make inferences, providing experiences that help build a strong knowledge base is important. Similarly,

Setting Individual Learning Goals

Student Name: __Alexandra__   Content: __Making Inferences (Reading)__

Characteristics	Student Response			Teacher Intervention		
	Low	Medium	High	Low	Medium	High
Has background knowledge	X					Provides experiences to build knowledge base
Exhibits independence in learning content	X					Provides models to scaffold independent practice
Applies abstract, higher-level thinking	X					Provides more support for thinking
Displays high level of autonomy			X	Uses more student-centered activities		
Follows complex instructions		X			Gives moderately complex instructions	
Masters learning at a rapid pace	X					Provides extended time

since Alexandra is "high" in autonomy, the teacher should ensure that she has independence and that some activities are self-directed. View the chart on page 77 to see the balance of student needs with a teacher response.

Alexandra's teacher realizes that Alexandra, who lives in a housing project in the city, has a limited understanding of animal habitats. One of the state science objectives asks students to *identify organisms that are dependent on one another in a given ecosystem and define habitat, explaining how a change in habitat affects an organism* (www.pdesas.org, 2010). Before talking about the habitats of mammals, birds, reptiles, or any other animal, the teacher primed Alexandra's thinking with a series of questions connecting the habitats she and her friends encountered in the city. The paved, fenced-in basketball court at the end of the block where her older brother hangs out, the church choir she sings in, and the drug store where she and her friends go to buy drinks and candy were all used to make connections. The teacher also modeled thinking about making connections by saying, "I make a connection between habitats and my car. I keep my car very clean and my habitat for driving includes my music CDs, my spare umbrella, my car deodorizer, and some bottled water. My husband's car habitat is very different. He keeps the empty drink cups and trash on the floor, his tennis shoes and workout clothes are in the back, newspapers are on the seat, and he likes the radio on all the time. When I think about the cars, I make a connection to different habitats of animals. I wonder if my car habitat is more like a mammal's habitat and my husband's car is more like a bird's habitat." The teacher asked Alexandra to look at several nonfiction readers about habitats and work on her own for a few minutes to find some connections between her environment and habitats of different animals, using a compare-and-contrast graphic organizer designed for the task.

The teacher then posed a series of inference questions to probe for thinking:

- What would happen if your brother no longer had a basketball court close by? How would his life change?

- What would happen if something significant changed in an animal habitat, such as a drought or someone coming in and clearing the woods to build houses?

- When you look at the picture in the book of the environment the snake lives in, what might occur to threaten its habitat?

Complex Thinking Is for *All* Students

A fellow teacher once said to me, "These thinking tasks are good for my regular and gifted kids, but the struggling students won't get it." Think of this: If we never provide opportunities for struggling learners to engage in complex thinking, how are they going to learn to make the complex decisions they will encounter throughout life? As you make decisions about clustering students for tiered instruction and choosing the strategies that support learning, remember that critical thinking and problem solving need to be practiced by all students!

The goal is to design instruction so students do *the work* of thinking. Support for thinking occurs when you prompt, prod, and guide students to reflect, extend, and grapple with more complex thinking. Consider the weaving metaphor below:

> The teacher works with each student's thinking, while weaving other students into the interchange of ideas. She is the master weaver, holding threads of important ideas and bringing them back to the surface when they're dropped. She has in mind a very general design for the weaving, which enables her to return to previous ideas in order to move the group's thinking along. The details of the design, however, are determined by students' input.
>
> (Hogan & Pressley, 1997, p. 91).

While there is general agreement that infusing higher-order thinking throughout lessons is a worthy goal, observation of classes has shown us that students are offered only sporadically questions and tasks that require them to think at higher levels (Redfield & Rousseau, 1981). Building higher-level thinking into classroom instruction is successful when you design the questions before you start the lesson. It definitely pays off to put time and effort in the "up-front" work of crafting quality questions to ensure that all students have opportunities for complex thinking, regardless of their entry levels. When you tier instruction, you must be intentional about creating opportunities to stretch each student's thinking. In this regard, make it a rule of thumb to give away as few answers as possible, so that students have the opportunity to work toward the answers themselves.

Below are several methods to prompt students as thinkers and may be used with small, tiered groups or the whole class.

Strategies to Prompt Student Thinking

- *Frame a problem or articulate a goal:* "It sounds to me that what you're talking about relates to the impact of global warming on life forms in the Arctic."

- *Refocus the discussion:* "We seem to agree on the first point. Let's consider the second statement and see how it influences our thinking."

- *Invite interaction of ideas:* "Who can build on Kala's ideas and expand our thinking?"

- *Asks for clarification:* "Can you tell me your evidence source or find support in the text for your comment that, 'Coastal cities will be submerged by rising sea water?'"

- *Ask for Elaboration:* "Can you explain a bit more about the comment you just made?"

(Adapted from Hogan & Pressley, 1997, p. 90)

As you plan a lesson, whether you are working with individual students or the whole class, you have a great deal of control over how you choose to engage students with higher-order questions. Linda Darling-Hammond (1997), a researcher and author on teaching and learning, distinguishes between work that keeps students busy and work that advances learning:

> Work that results in deep understanding has at least three features: it requires the use of higher-order cognitive functions, taking students beyond recall, recognition, and reproduction of information to evaluation, analysis, synthesis, and production of arguments, ideas, and performance. It asks students to apply these skills and ideas in meaningful contexts, engaging them in activities they have real reason to want to undertake. And it builds upon students' prior learning but presses toward more disciplined understandings. (p. 109)

Tiered Instruction:
Adjusting Questioning Strategies

Teacher Marsha Brubaker planned to present the following math problem to three students at varying levels:

In yesterday's lesson, I grouped a set of counters so that there were the same number of counters in each group. I can't remember how many were in each group, but I do know there were 12 counters all together. What might the groups have been?

Before presenting this problem, Marsha reflected on her students' potential responses; tiering instruction requires that we consider the complexity of thinking that students can handle and the kinds of questions we can pose to foster that thinking. Of the three students Martha planned to engage in this math task, Sam finds all the answers and can explain his responses quickly, Kate finds one answer and calls it "done," and Ryan struggles with a basic understanding of the problem. For these learners, the process definitely needs to be tiered; therefore, in anticipation of the students' responses, Marsha and her team members, Jane Lobb and Stephanie Haskins, brainstormed and recorded some questions for the varying levels of response anticipated:

Ryan (Group 3: Struggling with the task):

- What do you know in this problem?

- Can you show me with counters?

- When you listen to the problem, what do you picture in your mind?

- Is there a particular place that is confusing to you?

Kate (Group 2: Meeting the task, but could be expanded):

- Are there any other answers?

- Are there other ways you can show your answer?

- Can you create a similar problem?

Sam (Group 1: Needs expanded task):

- If I had 28 counters, would you solve the problem the same way?

- How would the problem be different?

- If I had 29 counters what occurs?

Differentiating With Divergent Questions

To further challenge students' thinking, it is important to build in opportunities for them to respond to divergent questions. These open-ended questions benefit learners because there is no "gotcha" effect, since students aren't asked to provide a single right answer. They are naturally differentiated because each student's response is individualized. The following questions focusing on earth science content provide examples:

- What words or phrases can you think of that might be used to describe a volcano in its various stages?
- What would happen if the earth's crust had no faults?
- How is a volcano like a temper tantrum?
- How is an earthquake like a traffic jam?

Open-ended is the operative term when using divergent questions. Reorganization questions consistently fall into this category. Excellent strategies include using "forced association" questions, which lead students to find connections between two things that are generally unalike, as well as questions that shift point of view in a novel and unusual way. Creative questions, such as challenging students to think of a familiar object—a yardstick, for example—and then think of alternate uses for it, are another type of open-ended question. Divergent questions can be used in whole-class instruction as well as with individuals and small groups, particularly when students respond independently and in writing. When you ask questions that lead students to tap into their ideas as opposed to questions that have one right answer, you are probing thinking at the student's level, while at the same time reducing fear of failure. For example, a fifth-grade teacher explains the task to his class:

> *Do you remember our conversation about using off-the-wall questions to get your brains to think harder? I called these questions divergent questions because they make us diverge—or think in many different directions. We are halfway through our unit on plate tectonics, and I want to review using some of these divergent questions. I want each of you to think on your own, so I will ask you to use the think page scratch paper on your desk. You have 90 seconds to write a response on the think page. You may list responses*

  A Practical Guide to Tiering Instruction in the Differentiated Classroom © 2010 by Sarah Armstrong, Scholastic Professional

or write them in full sentences. Here is our first question: How is a volcano like a temper tantrum? [He waits approximately 90 seconds.] Now, before we go on to another divergent question, talk to the people in your group and share one of your thoughts. The next question is a little different. It is called a reorganization question and gets you to think about what might happen if something were different than it usually is. You have 90 seconds to write one or two responses to this question: What would happen if the earth's crust had no faults?

Web sites that serve as a resource for divergent questions are:

http://www.virtualsalt.com/ crebook2.htm

http://www.mycoted.com/ Category:Creativity_Techniques

Divergent questions help students in each group make important connections that reinforce understandings of the term or concept. Not only do students feel that it is safe to respond, but they generally enjoy the creative twist associated with divergent questions. These questions support differentiation because students with varied background knowledge or a range of achievement levels can provide content-rich responses based on the knowledge they already possess. A key benefit of these questions lies in the fact that they don't have one right answer; rather, they ask students to employ skills of analysis and synthesis to reflect on many possible answers.

Managing the Process of Tiering

Teachers who are newly committed to differentiating for their students often ask, "Now that I'm a firm believer in the need to tier instruction, how do I structure my classroom to make it happen?" As previously noted, incorporating pre-assessment is essential, as is developing a clear grasp of the content students must learn. An important next step is to develop systems for efficiently managing the process of tiering. In short, you need to think of ways to organize your classroom to accommodate groups of students simultaneously working at different levels.

Materials that support cooperative learning strategies provide excellent ideas on placing students in like (homogeneous) or mixed (heterogeneous) work groups. In addition, Response to Intervention (RtI) Web sites, referred to in Chapter 1, provide ideas about managing tiered instruction.

Divergent Questions That Promote Higher-Order Thinking

English

- What would happen if books never used quotation marks for dialogue?
- How is reading a newspaper like planting a garden?
- How is *Alice's Adventures in Wonderland* like going to a shopping mall?

Social Studies

- You are the Mississippi River. What role have you played in settling North America?
- How is Martin Luther King, Jr., like an automobile?
- What would happen if Earth stopped rotating?

Science

- If you were the periodic table and nobody thought you were important, what would you say to convince them?
- How is a cell like a refrigerator?
- How is global warming like eating dinner at a fast food restaurant?

Math

- You are a cylinder. Describe how you have influenced today's world.
- How is solving an equation like riding the school bus each day?
- What would happen if the only numbers we had were Roman numerals?

Strategies for Assigning and Managing Tiered Tasks

Here I'll share some additional examples for setting up tiered lessons that teachers have successfully used to differentiate. One idea for communicating expectations for individual work is to provide specific task cards or folders that define the work of the day or week. Below are some variations of ways to communicate tasks to students:

Tent Cards

Card stock may be folded into varying forms (in half vertically or horizontally or into thirds to create a bottom). The task can be listed on one side of the card, and the directions on the other. This might be appropriate if the task does not involve any materials from the teacher.

Gift Bags

Gift bags can hold both directions and materials students will need to perform a particular task. This might be appropriate if the teacher needs to provide some bulky materials. In this case the task is to read a story and construct a scene in the story using the materials in the bag. Students are involved in language and spatial tasks with an added kinesthetic, hands-on piece as they construct the scene.

Tent cards

 Gift bags

Center Folders

Manila file folders may be designed with a title on the front, directions or task card on the left inside, and an activity sheet on the right side. This might be appropriate if the task involves additional handouts from the teacher. The example below shows three different colored folders which might be given to three different tiers.

Pocket Folders

Directions can be typed onto a full or half-sheet of paper. The directions are then glued to a 6- x 9-inch or 9- x 12-inch manila folder, with materials inserted. This might be appropriate if the task involves "loose" items, such as sorting cards, but may also be used for additional handouts. The first example below shows math task cards of varying colors, with one color representing on-grade-level tasks and another color representing above-grade-level tasks. The second example shows how instructions can be described directly on the front of the envelope.

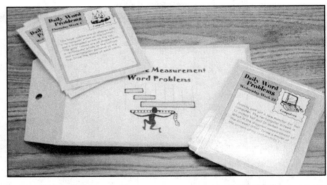

Center folders

Pocket folders

Tiering With Personal Agendas

Creating "personal agendas" is another efficient way to inform students about the learning goals you have identified for them. When using a personal agenda, outline steps of each activity for students. On pages 88–90, you will find examples of daily agendas developed by Carla VanDevander, a middle-school instructional coach, who uses this technique to differentiate for eighth-grade students. The category headings are aligned with several of the nine correlates of achievement that are discussed in *Classroom Instruction That Works* by Marzano, Pickering, and Pollock (2001). These authors cite research suggesting that students achieve at higher levels when they gain adeptness in these nine areas.

Notice that in these examples the learning goals are the same for all students, but are tiered to accommodate individual needs.

Supporting Student Learning Using Personal Agendas Based on the Nine Correlates of Achievement

Instructional Strategy	Definition
Setting objectives and providing feedback	Helping students understand the direction for learning and establish personal goals, and providing feedback about how they are progressing toward their goals
Questions, cues, and advanced organizers	Helping students retrieve what they know about a topic, using questions that elicit inferences, cues, or hints about what is to come
Identifying similarities and differences	Engaging students in activities that help them examine similarities and differences among ideas, issues, events, etc. by engaging in mental processes such as comparing, classifying, creating metaphors, and creating analogies
Cooperative learning	Using grouping strategies to help students in their learning
Nonlinguistic representations	Helping students represent and elaborate on knowledge in an imagery form using mental pictures, physical models, graphic organizers, etc.
Note taking/summarizing	Helping students distill and/or synthesize information accurately and concisely
Reinforcing effort and providing recognition	Teaching students about the relationship between effort and achievement and recognizing students for the progress they are making
Homework and practice	Providing students with opportunities to deepen their understanding of content and their proficiency and skills
Generating and testing hypotheses	Engaging students in activities that ask them to apply knowledge by generating and testing a hypothesis, such as problem solving, decision making, experimental inquiry, systems analysis, investigation, projects, etc.

(adapted from Classroom Instruction That Works *by Marzano, Pickering, and Pollock, 2001)*

Daily Agenda Example

Personal Agenda for Student ON Grade Level

Standard: Describe the roles and powers of the executive branch; explain the principles of checks and balances

1. Advance Organizer	2. Generate/Test Hypothesis	3. Nonlinguistic Representations
Anticipation guide on executive branch 1. Read the five statements on the anticipation guide. 2. In left-hand column under "Now" check "T" for true or "F" for false to check your understanding of the implied and explicit powers of the office of the president.	Brainstorm the role of the president to determine how our political system would be different if there were no check on the power of the executive branch. Use your textbook or other resources to complete the following tasks: 1. In a well-written paragraph, explain what you know about the powers of the executive branch. 2. In a well-written paragraph, explain the checks on the executive branch's powers and who or what checks them. Construct a hypothesis to determine what our country would be like if there were no limitations on presidential power.	Symbolize executive power by completing one of the following tasks: 1. Draw a political cartoon that illustrates a specific power of the president. 2. Draw a three-panel picture to symbolize three powers of the president.

4. Similarities and Differences	5. Summarizing and Note Taking	6. Closure
Compare and contrast our current president's powers to the powers of England's king during Colonial times by completing the following task: 1. Using a Venn diagram or compare-contrast thinking map, make a list of the differences and similarities between the presidency and the monarchy, based on the following points: term in office, limits on powers, powers, function.	Complete one of the following assignments to gauge understanding of the powers of the executive branch: 1. Summarize the powers of the president by constructing a short feature article on the implied and explicit powers of president. 2. Create a set of bulleted notes about the roles and responsibilities of the presidency, both implied and explicit.	Revisit the anticipation guide on the executive branch. • In the right-hand column under "Later" check "T" for true or "F" for false to see if your understanding of the implied or explicit powers of the office of the president has changed.

Daily Agenda Example

Personal Agenda for Student ABOVE Grade Level

Standard: Describe the roles and powers of the executive branch; explain the principles of checks and balances

1. Advance Organizer	2. Generate/Test Hypothesis	3. Nonlinguistic Representations
Anticipation guide on executive branch 1. Read the five statements on the anticipation guide. 2. In left-hand column under "Now" check "T" for true or "F" for false to check your understanding of the implied and explicit powers of the office of the president.	Brainstorm the role of the president to determine how our political system would be different if there were no check on the power of the executive branch. Use your textbook and other resources to construct an essay that includes discussion of: 1. implied powers of the presidency 2. the explicit powers of the presidency 3. who or what ensures that the checks and balances are adhered to Generate a hypothesis that determines what our country would be like if there were no limitations on presidential power.	Symbolize executive power by completing one of the following tasks: 1. Draw a political cartoon that illustrates a specific power of the president and include visual commentary on how the power is checked. 2. Locate and analyze a published political cartoon about presidential powers and create a new one that reflects a perspective that is in contrast to the cartoon you analyzed.

4. Similarities and Differences	5. Summarizing and Note Taking	6. Closure
Research a country that has a different leader and power structure, such as a dictatorship, and complete the following assignment: • Using a Venn diagram or format of your choice, list the differences and similarities between the presidency and the leadership structure of another government. Please include at least ten indicators to show your analysis.	Complete one of the following assignments to gauge understanding of the powers of the executive branch: 1. Summarize the powers of the president by constructing a short feature article on the implied and explicit powers of the president. 2. Design a lesson plan a teacher might use to teach about the powers of the executive branch.	Revisit the anticipation guide on the executive branch. • In the right-hand column under "Later" check "T" for true or "F" for false to see if your understanding of the implied or explicit powers of the office of the president has changed.

Daily Agenda Example

Personal Agenda for Student BELOW Grade Level

Standard: Describe the roles and powers of the executive branch; explain the principles of checks and balances

1. Advance Organizer	2. Generate/Test Hypothesis	3. Nonlinguistic Representations
Anticipation guide on executive branch 1. Read the five statements on the anticipation guide. 2. In left-hand column under "Now" check "T" for true or "F" for false to check your understanding of the implied and explicit powers of the office of the president.	Brainstorm the role of the president to determine how our political system would be different if there were no check on the power of the executive branch. Use your trade books and note sheets to complete the following tasks: 1. List the powers of the executive branch. 2. List checks and balances on the executive branch's powers and who or what checks them. 3. List the differences that you think our country would experience if there were no limitations on presidential power.	Symbolize executive power by completing one of the following tasks: 1. Draw a two-panel picture in which one panel illustrates a specific power of the president and the second panel illustrates how the power is checked. 2. Look at the folder of political cartoons and select two. Complete a compare-contrast thinking map graphic organizer on how the cartoons are alike and how they are different.
4. Similarities and Differences	**5. Summarizing and Note Taking**	**6. Closure**
Using the fact sheet that outlines current presidential powers and powers belonging to the king during Colonial times, compare and contrast our current president's powers to the powers of England's king by completing the following task: • Using a compare-contrast thinking map, make a list of the differences and similarities between the presidency and the monarchy, based on the following points: term in office, limits on powers, powers, function.	Complete one of the following assignments to gauge understanding of the powers of the executive branch: 1. Create a set of bulleted notes about the roles and responsibilities of the presidency. 2. Write a letter to the current president of the United States discussing the powers he now holds as president.	Revisit the anticipation guide on the executive branch • In the right-hand column under *Later* check "T" for true or "F" for false to see if your understanding of the implied or explicit powers of the office of the president has changed.

 A Practical Guide to Tiering Instruction in the Differentiated Classroom © 2010 by Sarah Armstrong, Scholastic Professional

Selecting Graphic Organizers for Tiered Instruction

Graphic organizers are tools that tap into both verbal and spatial (nonlinguistic) ways of thinking. When selecting a particular graphic organizer, it is helpful to consider the organizational strengths of your learners. To what degree are students able to process and organize information, and which graphic organizers will support them at their level of need?

Look again at the tiers for the topic of electricity discussed on page 72 to see how the graphic organizers were adapted. Notice the varying degrees of complexity in the graphic organizers on pages 73–74. The Group 1 graphic organizer requires students to organize information into two categories—either parallel or series circuits. The Group 2 graphic organizer adds complexity by requiring students to think about whether information worked or didn't work, provide reasons why, and classify circuits as parallel or series. Group 3 involves applying new vocabulary terms—*resistance, voltage,* and *current*—since prior assessment has revealed that students have a strong understanding of parallel and series circuits. Each of the graphic organizers offers scaffolds for students, based on levels of achievement.

In addition to graphic organizers specifically designed for a task, providing generic organizers that support different thinking skills is a good way to differentiate. You are probably quite familiar with the Venn diagram (page 92), but you can add complexity to that organizer by using a Multi-Venn (page 92) and having students determine similarities and differences among three things—for example, analyzing common and distinct attributes of three different poems. The Compare-Contrast Thinking Map on page 93 (www.readingquest.org/pdf/compare.pdf) readily supports a task for students at a lower entry level because you can provide more guidance on the desired outcome by filling in the "With Regard to" section. A completed Compare-Contrast Thinking Map (at right) examining warm and cold fronts illustrates its use. Note the visual images that are included to assist with recall.

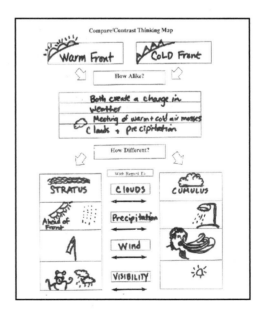

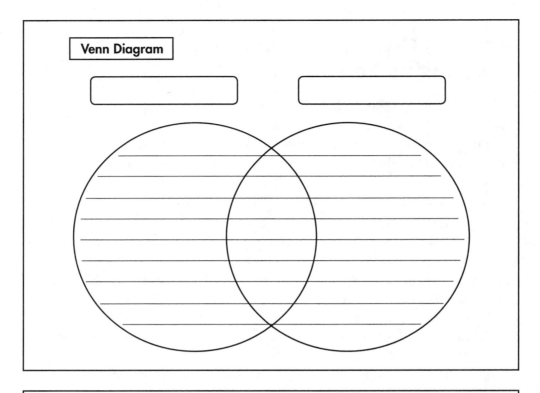

Venn Diagram

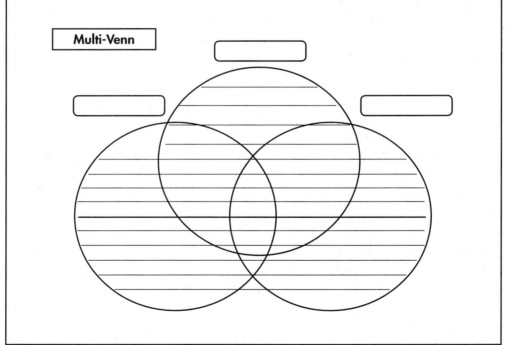

Multi-Venn

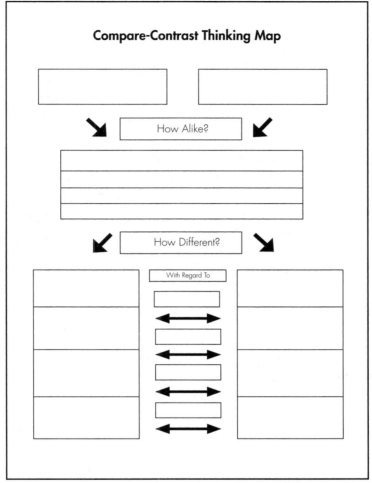

Adjusting Social Interaction

Most learners welcome opportunities to interact and engage with fellow students. The importance of socialization in the classroom extends to learning activities in addition to other nonacademic aspects of the school day. Engaging in tiered instruction leads to varying levels of social interaction in the classroom. For example, you might shift from whole-class interaction to small-group interaction and then back again. Students may work individually on tiered tasks and then might join together in centers or at stations to work on a task collectively.

Social interaction is not restricted to the students. Powerful differentiated instruction can be designed when groups of teachers work together to tier in cross-class grouping based on needs within a grade level or department team.

One way to tier process is through a jigsaw activity (Aronson, 2009). The basis of a jigsaw activity is to involve students in two groups, "expert" and "home." Each student in a home group is assigned an area for which he or she must become an "expert." All students designated as "experts" for a particular area work together to develop their expertise about the topic. Then experts return to their home group, where they share their knowledge and learn about other topics from other "experts." For example, let's revisit the leveled readers mentioned on page 61, which address this learning goal: *The student will investigate and understand that matter is anything that has mass, takes up space, and occurs as a solid, liquid, or gas.* The following leveled readers would allow students to work at five different tiers.

Leveled Readers for Tiered Instruction on Matter

Title/Author	Publisher	Fountas/Pinnell Level
What Is Matter?, by Lisa Trumbauer	Newbridge	Level J
My World of Science: Solids, Liquids, Gases, by Angela Royston	Heinemann	Level L
Ranger Rick: The World of Matter, by Ron Cole	Newbridge	Level N
Properties of Matter: Blue Planet Diaries, by Lisa Boehm	Newbridge	Level S
Science Concepts: Matter, by Alvin Silverstein, Virginia Silverstein, and Laura S. Nunn	Lerner	Level Y

In a jigsaw activity, small groups of students would be responsible for key information from their respective texts. Typically, the teacher would have task cards or a study guide to support students' interaction with different books and to guide thinking. After a designated length of time (no more than the age of the learner, as discussed in the lesson design chapter) students would do one of two things:

1. Return to the whole group and take turns debriefing their small-group responses to the class—either sharing this task or allowing a designated reporter to speak for the group.

2. Regroup from expert to home groups and have students share responses to their respective tasks with each other in small home groups while the teacher circulates, checking for understanding. In a jigsaw, students are able to read at varying levels, but remain focused on similar content and objectives. A strong benefit is the sharing and accountability component, which allows all students to contribute to the learning community within the classroom.

In the following example on weather, students were given a slip of paper that provided them with the title of the book that they were to use to help them complete the task. (These books were previously referenced in Chapter 4.) The example uses a class of 23 students. You will notice that the "reading" groups (represented by rows) have an unequal number since these are based on students' reading levels, which varies. However, the number in each of the "sharing" groups (represented in columns) is a similar size.

Using Books of a Range of Reading Levels to Jigsaw Content About Weather

Looking at Clouds by Susan Ring	*Looking at Clouds* by Susan Ring	*Looking at Clouds* by Susan Ring	*Looking at Clouds* by Susan Ring	*Looking at Clouds* = 4 students
Stormy Weather by Natalie Lunis	*Stormy Weather* by Natalie Lunis	*Stormy Weather* by Natalie Lunis	*Stormy Weather* by Natalie Lunis	*Stormy Weather* = 6 students
		Stormy Weather by Natalie Lunis	*Stormy Weather* by Natalie Lunis	
Weather Words by Gail Gibbons	*Weather Words* by Gail Gibbons	*Weather Words* by Gail Gibbons	*Weather Words* by Gail Gibbons	*Weather Words* = 7 students
Weather Words by Gail Gibbons	*Weather Words* by Gail Gibbons	*Weather Words* by Gail Gibbons		
And Now for the Weather! by William O'Byrne	*And Now for the Weather!* by William O'Byrne	*And Now for the Weather!* by William O'Byrne	*And Now for the Weather!* by William O'Byrne	*And Now for the Weather!* = 6 students
And Now for the Weather! by William O'Byrne	*And Now for the Weather!* by William O'Byrne			
6 in each sharing group	6 in each sharing group	6 in each sharing group	5 in each sharing group	23 students total

The title was very specific, depending upon the reading level of the students. However, each slip of paper was also color coded, and students randomly received one of four colors. Each student joined other students with the same book title, working within the group to become an "expert" in explaining the material. After an allotted amount of time, students then rejoined with students that had the same colors (home groups). Each student

---

Task Cards for Expert Groups Studying Weather

Group 1

You are a meteorologist, a scientist who studies the weather and uses what is known to predict the weather! Read the book *Looking at Clouds*. Explain the cause-and-effect relationship between clouds and weather. Create a visual or other representation to help explain this to your peers. You may use a four-square graphic organizer to help you explain this relationship, if needed.

Group 2

You are a meteorologist, a scientist who studies the weather and uses what is known to predict the weather! Read the book *Stormy Weather*. Explain the cause-and-effect relationship between wind and weather. Create a visual or other representation to help explain this to your peers. You may use mnemonics and drawings to help explain this relationship.

Group 3

You are a meteorologist, a scientist who studies the weather and uses what is known to predict the weather! Read the book *Weather Words*. Explain the cause-and-effect relationship between temperature and fronts, and weather. Create a visual or other representation to help explain this to your peers. You may use mnemonics and drawings to help explain this relationship.

Group 4

You are a meteorologist, a scientist who studies the weather and uses what is known to predict the weather! Read the book *And Now for the Weather!* Explain the cause-and-effect relationship between air pressure and weather. Create a visual or other representation to help explain this to your peers. You may use mnemonics and drawings to help explain this relationship.

helped "teach" others within the group about the content. After all students had shared, students were then held accountable by being asked to document what they had learned.

Through the jigsaw, each student was able to access the content and reach the lesson objective. Because of the slightly varying content within the texts, students were also able to contribute information that was new to their classmates.

Cooperative Learning Resources to Support Teaching and Learning

Partner or group cooperative learning activities give students opportunities to work in mixed-tier groups or at the same tier level. Excellent sources for a wide range of cooperative learning activities include:

The Jigsaw Classroom: Building Cooperation in the Classroom, 2nd edition (1997) by Elliott Aronson and S. Patnoe, New York: Addison Wesley Longman.

Cooperation in the Classroom, 7th edition. (1998) by David and Roger Johnson and Edythe Holubec. Edina, MN: Interaction Book Company.

Kagan Cooperative Learning by Spencer Kagan & Miguel Kagan, Kagan Publishing.

The Cooperative Learning Network, http://www-acad.sheridanc.on.ca/scls/coop/cooplrn.htm

The International Association for the Study of Cooperation in Education (IASCE) http://www.iasce.net/index.html

The Cooperative Learning Center at the University of Minnesota, http://www.co-operation.org

---

Summary

As a teacher, you have artistic license to create lessons that work effectively with your students at their level of need. You choose the tools, the medium and the canvas for each of your students. Through your efforts to differentiate by process, students will start at different points, use materials specific to their learning goals, and develop products unique to their achievement levels.

Ideas for Reflection

1. Read the questions on page 68 at the beginning of this chapter under the heading "How Will I Engage Students?" How frequently do you address these questions when you plan a lesson? Which questions are easiest to address? Which are more difficult?

2. Look at the chart "Differentiating by Process: Teacher Role" on page 70. Use the chart to work on your own or with a colleague to plan a specific lesson or unit of instruction that is differentiated for students.

3. Consider how you incorporate higher-order thinking questions in your lessons. Do you consistently probe for thinking—getting students to do the *work of thinking*? Do you use divergent questioning strategies to encourage all students to develop creative and critical thinking skills? Be intentional over the next few weeks about planning lessons that encourage thinking.

4. What graphic organizers do you use most frequently? In what ways do they differentiate for your students while still emphasizing the same content?

5. How have you differentiated the products students are required to produce to show evidence of what they know? What rubrics or criteria have you provided so students know the requirements of the project?

Chapter 6

Product: Tiering Ways Students Demonstrate What They Know

Have you ever stepped into a self-serve shoe store with the intention of finding the perfect shoe for an upcoming special event? First you find the section featuring your size, because the style doesn't really matter if the shoe doesn't fit. Then you examine the selection of shoes while searching for the pair that works for your occasion: Cool summer casuals? Dress shoes to match evening wear? Cleats for the soccer match? Your goal is to find the shoes that are suitable for the event.

Developing tiered assessments can be likened to searching for the perfect pair of shoes. The teacher's task is to provide students with assessments that are the right fit, having an appropriate degree of difficulty while effectively addressing the content that's been taught. An essential aim in the process is to design assessments in which students are able to show what they know and can do, but which also provide students with sufficient success to feel confident enough to move forward. There is no one-shoe-fits-all formula for finding this match, so differentiating the work students produce and the manner in which they are assessed is essential.

Carol Tomlinson likes to say, "There is nothing so unequal as treating unequals equally" as a way of highlighting the importance of differentiating by content, process, and product. It's not unusual for teachers to do a double take when they hear Tomlinson's comment because it implies that it is a good thing to not make every child do the same thing in the same way. At times teachers argue the opposing view, saying that it isn't fair to other students if one child reads an easier book or has fewer vocabulary words—or is assessed with a different test. However, if seeing our learners progress is the goal, then providing students with tiered assessments that fit their needs is entirely appropriate.

Expanding Perspectives About Assessment

A balance of assessment measures are needed to effectively inform teaching and guide thinking of students. Jay McTighe and Steven Ferrara (1998) created a "Framework of Assessment Approaches and Methods" that reflect the broad spectrum of possibilities included in both selected-response and constructed-response formats; see chart on page 101.

I discussed assessment in Chapter 2 with an emphasis on pre-assessment and self-assessment. Talking about assessment as an end product—that is, a test or grade—will be addressed here. Assessment options span a wide spectrum. However, the use of selected response assessments that include multiple choice, true-false, and short-answer responses is predominant in today's classrooms. These tests— generally perceived as efficient, easier to grade, and more objective—have the potential to confine critical thinking, creativity, and relevant application of new learning.

Once you understand the broad range of assessments from which you can draw, selecting a testing format and adapting it to the specific needs of your students can be accomplished more readily. At this point decisions must be made regarding differentiating assessment for different tiers of students. The example below provides a framework for thinking about offering assessment options for several standards.

Teachers typically measure what students know by reviewing the products they generate. These products are derived from tasks children do to practice or demonstrate understanding of the content: graphic organizers, interactive journals, study guides, projects, worksheets, oral presentations, group dialogue, homework, quizzes, tests, and so on. Tomlinson (1999) defines the product as "a vehicle through which a student shows (and extends) what he or she has come to understand and can do as a result of a considerable segment of learning" (p. 43).

A Practical Guide to Tiering Instruction in the Differentiated Classroom © 2010 by Sarah Armstrong, Scholastic Professional

Framework of Assessment Approaches and Methods

Constructed-Response Format

Performance-Based Assessment

Selected-Response Format	Brief Constructed Response	Product	Performance	Process-Focused Assessment
• Multiple-choice	Fill in the blank	• Essay	• Oral presentation	• Oral questioning
• True-false	• word(s)	• Research paper	• Dance/movement	• Observation "kid watching"
• Matching	• phrase(s)	• Story/play	• Science lab demonstration	• Interview
• Enhanced multiple choice	Short answer	• Poem	• Athletic skills performance	• Conference
	• sentence(s)	• Portfolio	• Dramatic reading	• Process description
	• paragraph	• Interactive notebook	• Enactment	• "Think aloud"
	Label a diagram	• Art exhibit	• Debate	• Learning log
	"Show your work"	• Science project	• Musical recital	
	Visual representation	• Model	• *Technology applications*	
	• web	• Video/audiotape	• Teach a lesson	
	• concept map	• Spreadsheet		
	• flow chart	• Lab report		
	• graph/table			
	• illustration			

Adapted from McTighe & Ferrara (1998)

What Are the Options for Assessment?

Learning Goal	Assessment Methods				Assessment Options
	Selected Response	Constructed Response	Performance Assessment	Personal Communication	
U.S. History: The student will demonstrate knowledge of the changing role of the United States from the late nineteenth century through World War I by explaining the reasons for and results of the Spanish-American War.		X		X	Written response or oral interview: • What were the reasons for the Spanish-American War? • What were the results of the Spanish-American War?
Reading: The student will identify cause- and-effect relationships.	X				Options for selected response work samples: • Highlight cause (in one color) & effect (in another color) within a text. • Match cause with effect (using paper/pencil format or kinesthetic sort). • Answer multiple-choice question.
Geometry: The student will make a model of a three-dimensional figure from a two-dimensional drawing and make a two-dimensional representation.			X		Pictures of student product/checklists/rubrics: Use of media for 3-D model may vary.

Note that homework, quizzes, and tests are just a portion of the information that informs a teacher about student learning. Such assessments are not to be thought of as a one-time event, but as a process. If you assess and realize that many of your students did not master the content as you had hoped, your immediate next step is to plan for reteaching and the next assessment. Since mastery is the goal, the teach-reteach cycle is continuous.

The key to developing any product or assessment is to be intentional about how it is developed. Use the checklist on page 103 to reflect on an assessment you have recently given.

Is Your Assessment On Target for Students? An Assessment Checklist

Directions: Use the indicators below to evaluate the project, paper, product, or test that you are using to measure what students have learned.

Indicator	Yes	No	What Change Is Needed?
Alignment			
Is the assessment authentic, including real-life connections and big ideas that demonstrate a depth of understanding?			
Does the assessment include specific vocabulary related to the content?			
Does the assessment align with the Look Fors or criteria lists that were provided to students?			
Does the method of assessing align with the verb—i.e., compare/contrast, analyze—as well as the level of thinking implied by the standard that is being assessed?			
Thinking Skills			
Does the assessment or product students complete reflect a range of complexity in thinking?			
Am I asking students to demonstrate a progression of thinking, moving from lower levels (knowledge, comprehension) to higher levels (analysis, evaluation, synthesis)?			
Appropriate Learner "Fit"			
Have students been offered choices?			
Are assessments tailored to the strengths and needs of my students?			
Informative			
Does the assessment incorporate self-check and feedback?			
Does the assessment inform my instruction? In what way(s)?			
Are there areas that I could adapt so the assessment is more effective for my students?			
Overall Test Development			
Is the assessment or required product a highly effective way to measure attainment of learning goals?			

Authentic Assessments

If learning is enhanced when information is authentic, teachers should model this goal through their assessments as well. Think about what a professional reader, writer, mathematician, scientist, or historian would do to show his or her understanding. Most likely he or she would share understanding in a book or article written to a particular audience, or solve a real mathematical problem, or summarize the results of an investigation in a report, or illustrate discovered artifacts in a portfolio or exhibit. We should use this lens to think about assessment as well. Rarely, if ever, are professionals completing worksheets to show what they know.

Martha Ratliff, an English teacher in Virginia, designed a performance task for students that tied to the citizenship ceremony that occurs each Fourth of July at Monticello, the home of Thomas Jefferson. The students actually lived in the area and had the opportunity to attend the naturalization ceremony. The task for students was to prepare art work, written work, and/or a dramatic presentation that could potentially be displayed in an exhibit at the ceremony, that communicates stories about the life of immigrants as they pursue the hope

Immigration Project With Authentic Assessment

The "Immigrant and Identity Project" was developed by Martha Ratliff to assess her students as they immersed themselves in the study of immigration.

Performance Task: The Fourth of July celebration at Monticello in Charlottesville, Virginia, will include student work and performance concerning the identity and lives of immigrants. Your English class has been invited to exhibit art work, written work, and/or perform a dramatic presentation. Your study of characterization, conflict, and the immigrant identity should reflect ways immigration has influenced the development of our country. You may pick a time period between 1892 (Ellis Island opens) and the present. You may chose from the following:

Visual Art: Create a poster or collage to illustrate the personality of an actual immigrant you have researched or a fictional one you have read about, reflecting on his or her life before and after immigration. Use quotations interspersed with your work to give the person a "voice." (Look at *The Arrival,* by Shaun Tan or *At Ellis Island,* by Louise Peacock, to see examples.)

Written Work: Interview a family member or community member who has parents or grandparents who immigrated to America. You may conduct the interview in person or by e-mail. Write the immigrant's story as if you were the person who immigrated. You may choose a diary format or letters written to family back home. Read *At Ellis Island,* by Louise Peacock, for ideas.

Dramatic Presentation: Create a dialogue between two intergenerational characters, imagining one person as the immigrant. You may choose which person is young and which is old. Address the following questions as you create a dialogue and write a script: What questions will one ask of the other? What conflicts will an immigrant find coming to the United States? Are there stories of hardship in getting here? How is culture and ethnicity a factor in the immigrant settling into a new country? (Look at Anna Deavere Smith's dramatic performance in *On the Road: A Search for American Character.*)

Assessment "Look Fors"

For all work:

1. The presentation of the character is understandable to the viewer, reader, or listener.
2. The historical background portrayed is accurate.
3. Character growth is shown by more than a collection of facts.
4. The complexity of the character is explored in relation to the experience and challenges of immigration.
5. The character shows development over time or in response to a major conflict.
6. All creative work follows the standard for the selected method of presentation.

Visual Art: Illustrations must be well chosen and reflect the theme. The overall presentation should be colorful and dynamic. The space should be full, using both quotations and pictures. Empty space should have a purpose.

Written Work: The interview should have seven to ten questions. The format selected for presenting the information should reveal the character, his/her culture, personal traits, concerns, emotions, and so on. The product should be well written and effectively communicate the story to the reader.

Dramatic Interpretation: The presentation must be true to life. The audience must believe that they are meeting someone from another cultural background. The dialogue should reveal the immigrant experience. Humor or pathos in the dialogue should be used effectively to engage the audience.

Source: Martha Stewart-Ratliff

of becoming a citizen of the United States. The task met required learning goals, yet asked students to reflect using fiction and nonfiction stories that communicated an authentic story.

Adapting Assessments to Students' Strengths

As you consider how to design optimal assessments, keep in mind that students often produce a higher quality of work if the assessment taps into a strength modality. It is not always appropriate or possible to create a test that aligns with a preferred way of learning, but doing so when possible establishes a balance of assessment methods. The chart below shows some of the possibilities framed in the language of multiple intelligences (Thomas Armstrong, 2003).

Matching Assessment With Students' Strengths

Verbal/Linguistic	Logical/Mathematical	Visual/Spatial
Speeches	Puzzles	Sorts
Storytelling	Problem solving	Artwork
Reading responses	Pattern analysis	Models
Written responses	Graphic organizers	Graphic organizers
Bodily/Kinesthetic	**Musical**	**Interpersonal**
Games	Songs	Jigsaws
Role playing	Jingles	Interviews
Presentations	Lyric poems	Conferences
Learning centers	Choral reading	Think-pair-share
Interpersonal	**Naturalistic**	**Existential**
Learning logs	Sorts	Debates
Self-evaluation	Diagrams	Concept maps
Research projects	Lab reports	Research projects
Reflective journals	Pattern analysis	Reflective journals

A Practical Guide to Tiering Instruction in the Differentiated Classroom © 2010 by Sarah Armstrong, Scholastic Professional

Providing "Look Fors" for Students

Measuring student progress is only meaningful if students are informed about the criteria on which they are being judged; otherwise, a test can be primarily

Guidelines for Creating Look Fors

These guidelines for creating Look Fors can assist you as you decide what tasks or projects need a list of criteria describing what constitutes high-quality work or a rubric outlining a continuum of quality.

Why Look Fors?
Students perform at their highest levels when they have a clear understanding of the expectations teachers have for them. Criteria lists or Look Fors for class work and projects guide students and serve as tools of self-reflection, eliminating uncertainty.

How often?
Teachers have asked, "Do I have to develop Look Fors for every assignment?" No. If a math teacher asks students to do the odd questions at the end of a chapter, Look Fors are not necessary. If the same teacher asks students to complete an illustrated poster of the real-life uses of three kinds of triangles, Look Fors are needed. Frequency will depend on the product or performance students are asked to deliver. But err on the side of having a criteria list—even if the list is short.

When are Look Fors essential?
Develop criteria lists or Look Fors for assignments any time the assignment has two or more components. Look Fors are also needed when you want to assess a range of skills such as organization, illustrations, format, and neatness. In addition, use Look Fors when the task is cumulative and you need to outline specific elements you want included.

Are Look Fors just for students?
No, clear expectations are important for teachers as well. Creating Look Fors for setting up a writer's workshop, excellence in a math classroom, or brain-compatible instruction can support teachers in their professional growth.

Is there a standard format?
Look Fors typically have the criteria on the left and a recording system on the right. The criteria can be in statement or question format.

a "gotcha" experience. Think of the end-of-the-year field day during which an array of activities and contests are being held. If you think you are competing in the long jump, but when you arrive at your event it is actually a half-mile run, you will likely not be prepared for the competition. Similarly, a major disconnect occurs if a student knows there is going to be a history test and expects questions on the geography of North America, but the test focuses on economics. Establishing the criteria or Look Fors with which a product or performance will be assessed is an essential step. See the chart on page 107 for guidelines on creating Look Fors.

Students as Partners in Assessment

In Chapter 2, I discussed several ways that students can self-assess as a pre-assessment. As an additional way to involve students in measuring their own progress, ask them to help establish Look Fors. It is a great way to increase ownership in both the learning task and assessment while at the same time ensuring that students review the criteria for the task. Another benefit is that it reduces the likelihood of the "I didn't know it was going to be on the test" response. Here are some examples:

- Students review the first three chapters of the shared novel that was read in English class and identify three to five key points in the story that drive the action. The teachers and students select the most significant actions and dissect them to gain additional insight. These insights, agreed upon by the students, become Look Fors that will be assessed.

- Students work in pairs to identify ten key facts of the American Revolution. As a group, the teacher and students compile the 20 most important facts/concepts. These items are the Look Fors that must be evident in a project on the time period.

- Each student writes down six goals that he or she must meet to have a well-organized, appropriately written science report. This personal list is added to in a conference with the teacher for a total of ten. These ten Look Fors become the criteria to be met by the individual student.

- The teacher provides students with an "I Can" list for a space science unit. The students monitor the list as they work on the assignments.

The teacher reviews the "I Can" survey with students to determine strengths and areas to improve.

Creating Self-Assessments

Self-assessments are varied and in many ways limitless. Although there are no formulas, here are a few suggestions to keep in mind.

- Create a culture of self-assessment in the classroom. Design a lesson focused on self-assessment explaining to students that the most meaningful learning experiences occur when they take responsibility for what they need to know and resolve to learn it. Show them different kinds of self-assessment. Ask them to come up with additional ways. Tell your students that you will frequently be asking them to self-assess.

- Stick to your commitment to build self-assessment into your instruction by being intentional about making it a part of your lesson design. If you are creating the "culture" with your students, you should use self-assessment several times a week.

- Use what you have. Once you develop an "I Can" checklist or other Look Fors, you can begin to create a notebook of resources for future classes. In addition, detailed checklists are often available in materials provided with textbooks.

Rubrics

I've mentioned the importance of creating Look Fors and the benefit of identifying criteria that guide both student tasks and assessment. An additional tool for both teachers and students is a rubric. Rubrics typically outline all aspects of a task or assignment that must be met in order to reach a certain level. You can find excellent resources for rubrics that both you and your students can use to assess at http://www.tcet.unt.edu/START/instruct/general/rubrics.htm.

There are two types of rubrics—analytical and holistic. Analytical rubrics are generally in a matrix format with specific performance subcategories identified, as illustrated in the example of the Earth-Moon-Sun Model below.

Self-Assessment of Space

Check the box below to show how you would rate yourself on each of these skills.

I Can . . .	Yes	Somewhat	Not there yet
I can tell and show the difference between rotation and revolution.			
I can tell about what causes the seasons.			
I can make a model that shows the phases of the moon in the correct order.			
I can tell how moon phases happen.			
I can tell about the sun's size, color, age, and what it is made of.			
I can tell how the surface of Earth, the moon, and the sun are the same and how they are different.			
I can make a model of Earth, the moon, and the sun that shows the differences in sizes and distance.			
I can compare the sizes and distances of Earth, the moon, and the sun.			
I can tell how an Earth-centered model and sun-centered model are the same and how they are different.			
I can tell what Aristotle, Ptolemy, Copernicus, and Galileo observed.			
I can tell the differences in what they observed.			
I can tell how they supported their conclusions.			
I can tell how the NASA missions have helped people understand the moon.			

A Practical Guide to Tiering Instruction in the Differentiated Classroom © 2010 by Sarah Armstrong, Scholastic Professional

Rubric for Earth-Moon-Sun Model

Check the box below to show how you would rate yourself on each of these skills.

Criteria	4 Exceeds Expectations	3 Meets Expectations	2 In Progress	1 Needs Improvement
Approximate scale distance	Distance has been calculated using accurate measurements and measuring tools, which is demonstrated in model and/or description.	Both the model and description show approximate scale distances.	Either the model or description shows incorrect scale distances.	Neither the model nor description shows approximate scale distances.
Approximate scale size	Size has been calculated using accurate measurements and measuring tools, which is demonstrated in model and/or description.	Both the model and description show approximate scale sizes.	Either the model or description shows incorrect scale sizes.	Neither the model nor description shows approximate scale sizes.
Appropriate characteristics	Both the model and description show more than two appropriate characteristics of Earth, the moon, and the sun.	Both the model and description show at least two appropriate characteristics of Earth, the moon, and the sun.	Either the model or description shows incomplete or incorrect characteristics of Earth, the moon, and the sun.	Neither the model nor description shows appropriate characteristics.
Appropriate motions	In addition to the appropriate motions of Earth, the moon, and the sun, the causes for seasons, moon phases, and tides are explained.	Both the model and description show appropriate motions of Earth, the moon, and the sun.	Either the model or description shows incomplete or incorrect motions of Earth, the moon, and the sun.	Neither the model nor description shows appropriate motions.

Holistic Rubric

Holistic Rubric for Primary Document Project

4 *Exceeds Expectations*	• Student conveys all aspects of the contrasting perspectives of the two groups. • Student provides deep analysis of three (3) primary sources. • Student clearly demonstrates persuasive writing and knowledge of subject matter. • Student clearly demonstrates knowledge of content by exemplary debating in class. • Student clearly displays evaluative thinking and critical analysis on the topic.
3 *Meets Expectations*	• Student addresses nearly all aspects of contrasting perspectives of the group. • Student uses two (2) out of three (3) primary sources • Student demonstrates persuasive writing, but lacks elaboration • Student makes some key points during debate. • Student explains and supports contrasting perspectives, but some information is lacking.
2 *In Progress*	• Student hits on a few key points, but it is clear there are holes in the assigned task. • Student uses one primary resource. • Student demonstrates persuasive writing but lacks insight and elaboration. • Student offers a few points during debate but leaves gaps. • Student does not demonstrate depth of thinking and lacks critical analysis.
1 *Needs Improvement*	• Student work and knowledge are extremely lacking and contrasting perspectives are not present, or if present, are not clearly stated. • Student uses one or no primary source. • Student has marginal written work. • Student is unable to debate on any aspect of the contrasting perspectives. • Work shows that student does not understand concept.

The holistic rubric organizes specific indicators across all categories according to the level of accomplishment attained by the students. An example of a holistic rubric created by teacher Jason Orrock for a fifth-grade classroom addresses the standard requiring students to analyze contrasting perspectives of Native Americans and settlers in regard to westward expansion. In addition, students are to develop skills in discussion and debate.

After Look Fors and/or rubrics have been developed, they can be adapted for tiered groups. For a student at an enrichment level, additional criteria might be added to enhance the task; similarly, for a student at a lower point of entry, the Look Fors might be selectively reduced. Some teachers build in the modifications and distribute Look Fors on color-coded paper to indicate tier levels.

Coaching Students With Self-Assessments

In many ways, using a variety of self-assessment tools can make your life easier because you have made students partners in the process. Self-assessments help make students responsible for their own learning. When students identify the criteria for an assignment, you are able to reinforce their involvement and the quality of their product with the following sorts of comments:

- (To an individual student) "Thank you for the assignment, James. Before I accept it I want you to review the Look Fors that we agreed on and make sure that you have met them all. We can talk about areas where you might not be sure and I will give you more time if need be."

- (To a class two days before a project is due) "Class, be sure to look at the criteria sheet that I gave you for the assignment. Check the yes or no column for each of the ten items. Remember, you get credit for being accurate in your own analysis of your project."

- (To any individual or group) "Yesterday we reviewed the content of the unit on explorers. You worked in small groups and came up with ten important facts and three concepts. As a class, we compiled the small-group information, coming up with 20 facts and five concepts. Here is the study guide based on your contributions. The test will be tomorrow and all information that you will need to know is in the study guide."

Incorporating Student Choice Into Assessment Design

Offering choice increases student ownership. Tomlinson and McTighe (2006) emphasize that "[e]ducators must be judicious in determining when it is important to offer product and performance options (and how many should be offered), striking a balance between a single path and a maze of options" (p. 77). There may be cases when there is only one way for a student to show what he or she knows. For example, if a standard states that students will "write a narrative report," then the operative task is for students to construct written work. While a partner activity using a graphic organizer may help generate content, ultimately the student still needs to *write*. Many times, however, a specific way of demonstrating knowledge is not required and you can build in choices for students.

A tiered assessment in a language arts class asks students to demonstrate the same essential understandings but with options for differing learning styles. In this approach the "what" remains the same, but the "how" depends on the learner. The example on page 115 taps into interest levels and multiple intelligences, allowing students to choose a modality on the left-hand side based on his or her preference and with the performance of the task(s) identified on the right-hand side. Even though the options are different, students are assessed with the same checklist or rubric criteria, since the essential understandings are the same. Third-grade teachers Courtney Chapman, Karen Peterson, Sara Vines, and Tammy Sanford and differentiation specialist Stephanie Haskins each contributed an activity, helping to create a menu for students that offers them choice.

Tiered Assessment in Language Arts

Reading Standard: Describe the images created by language.
Students select one option from the choices below to demonstrate their ability to describe images created by language.

"I love to write!" **Writer's Den**	Tammy read *When I'm Sleepy,* by Jane R. Howard, with students and asked them to think about the language from the story, paying special attention to sensory details. Students highlighted words related to sight, sound, smell, feel, and taste, and discussed how these words helped create images and deepen comprehension. Then the students wrote a piece on how the sensory images worked in the story.
"I love to build!" **Construction Area**	Stephanie paper-clipped pages at the end of *Big Mama's,* by Donald Crews, and directed students to stop reading when they reached the pages. At that point, students paused to discuss. Then they were given a printed card that contained the text of the last few pages only—no images. The students then used miscellaneous materials (blocks, newspaper, string, film canisters, tape, etc.) from the "Technology Toolbag" to model the scene as they thought it would appear. They then justified their scene by using words from the passage. After constructing, the students then compared their scene with the author's image in the last few pages.
"I love to act!" **Theater Corner**	Karen read the book *Twilight,* by Holly Young Huth, with students. She asked students to think about the character and how she was feeling at different points during the story, supporting their response with language from the story. She also asked how the character's feelings may have affected her facial expression and tone of voice. With a partner, students selected an excerpt from the story and practiced acting out the scene, focusing on the language to help determine actions and expressions.
"I love to draw!" **Artist's Studio**	Courtney had paper-clipped the last scene of *The Salamander Room,* by Anne Mazer, before reading it with students. Throughout the reading, students were asked to think about the images that "popped" into their minds and discuss how the language supported those images. When Courtney got to the last page, she read the words only and did not reveal the images. Then she gave students materials to make a pop-up book by folding a piece of white paper in half, cutting two slits on the fold, "popping" out along the slits, and then gluing a piece of construction paper backing (being careful not to put glue on the "popped out" portion). Students were given an index card to draw the image they visualized from hearing the last scene. They then glued the drawing to the popped out portion. On the other white space of the paper, they wrote key words or drew images that reflected what they heard, saw, smelled, or felt during the scene.
"I love to talk!" **Book Talk Zone**	Sara had typed a portion of the story *Night in the Country,* by Cynthia Rylant, onto posters for students. Students partnered together to read the story. Then students were given a graphic organizer and asked to record ideas about the mental image, picture, or movie scene that came to mind under the section of the organizer titled *My Image.* Students then talked about the images that they had drawn with a partner, explaining how they used the language from the story to draw the picture. After having a conversation and comparing the similarities and differences among pictures, students then made changes or additions to their image based on the use of language.

Note: Title of choices adapted from *Mosaic of Thought by Keene and Zimmerman, 1997.*

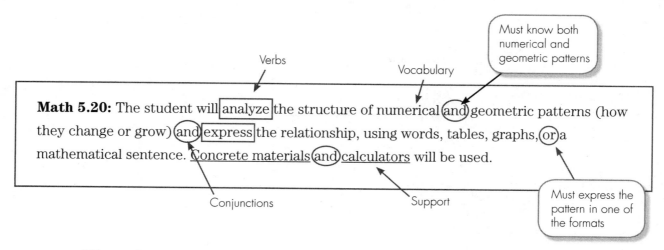

Verbs

Vocabulary

Must know both numerical and geometric patterns

Math 5.20: The student will analyze the structure of numerical and geometric patterns (how they change or grow) and express the relationship, using words, tables, graphs, or a mathematical sentence. Concrete materials and calculators will be used.

Conjunctions

Support

Must express the pattern in one of the formats

Tips for Developing Assessments

Teacher-generated assessments have the potential to be more closely aligned to standards than published assessments because teachers are able to carefully examine the verbs, vocabulary, and big idea using a specific, identified standard. As seen in Chapter 4, analysis of the verb should cue the teacher to the best testing format. Based on the verb, what might be a meaningful way to assess?

Let's return to the standard with a teacher's think-aloud about her analysis of this math standard:

"When I see the verb analyze, *I realize that this is a higher level of Bloom's taxonomy and will require students to look at something very closely, possibly break it apart, and make observations about what they observe. As an assessment for the verb* analyze, *I would require students to provide either a written or oral statement that explains their thinking. The written component might be in the form of diagrams, words, and so on.*

The chart on page 117 shows examples of verbs that might be in a standard and the possible impact on the type of assessment that you design.

As you expand your repertoire of how you test, keep in mind that the best assessment measures for the higher level of Bloom's revised taxonomy mentioned previously (Anderson & Krathwohl, 2001) are in the area of constructed-response items. As you begin to strive for a balance of assessment methods, decreasing methods that use selected-response and increasing those in the performance area should be a goal. The chart on page 118 approximates the connection between Bloom and assessment types.

Analyzing the Standards: Focus on Verbs

Verb	Implication	Possible Assessments
Describe	Implies written or verbal statement	• written or taped description • drawing and labeling • interactive notebook
Identify	Implies selecting from a group (selected response assessment would address)	• matching and labeling • A–Z chart • graphic organizer • word sort and picture sort • highlight • listing and drawing • picture of students pointing to item • interactive notebook
Compare	Implies making a judgment on likenesses and differences	• written or oral presentation • applying in graphic organizers • analyzing two or more works, pictures, indicators, graphs • debate or editorial
Create	Implies making something on own	• producing in writing or digitally • developing and completing projects • performing • designing products • drawing and modeling • presenting • diagramming • problem finding and problem solving
Interpret	Implies written or verbal summary	• producing in writing or digitally • creating an appropriate graphic organizer • making connections to related content • performing or demonstrating
Investigate	Implies hands-on investigation and/or experiment	• using research tools • writing steps (tape or tell) • problem solving • manipulating artifacts, objects • presenting findings • experimenting • outlining procedures: measure, classify, predict, test

Designing Assessments Based on Level of Thinking Skill

Bloom's Revised Taxonomy	Sample Verbs	Assessment Options
Remembering	find, identify, locate, match, recognize	Selected response
Understanding	describe, explain, recall, summarize	Selected response Constructed response Personal communication
Applying	demonstrate, predict, solve, use	Performance assessment Constructed response Personal communication
Analyzing	analyze, compare, differentiate, infer, investigate	Performance assessment Constructed response Personal communication
Evaluating	conclude, confirm, decide, determine, evaluate, justify	Constructed response Personal communication
Creating	construct, create, design, develop, plan	Performance assessment

Tiering: Providing Support and Extension

Tiering products used for assessment is very similar to tiering process to gauge how we might increase or decrease intensity as seen in the Scaffolding Readiness Scale on page 28. We first think about the standard, and then consider the options for assessment. For example, if the teacher's goal is to develop students' creativity, a multiple-choice or other selected-response

A Practical Guide to Tiering Instruction in the Differentiated Classroom © 2010 by Sarah Armstrong, Scholastic Professional

test will not serve the purpose. Similarly, it is a challenge to verify whether students can apply information they have learned through a selected-response assessment. Matching the assessment to the level of thinking you want students to demonstrate is essential.

Tiered Products With the Same Content

History Standard: The student will demonstrate knowledge of European exploration in North America by describing the motivations, obstacles, and accomplishments of the Spanish, French, Portuguese, and English explorations.

Advanced Learner: Have the student create a matrix that shows how the motivations, obstacles, and accomplishments of the Spanish, French, Portuguese, and English explorations compared and contrasted in North America and West Africa.

On-level Learner: Have student complete a matrix. The top of the matrix should include the terms *motivations, obstacles,* and *accomplishments.* The side of the matrix should include the names *Spanish, French, Portuguese,* and *English.* The student will be asked to use his own words in the spaces.

Struggling Learner: Provide support for completing the matrix listed for the on-level learner. Provide a word bank if the student needs language support, allow the student to arrange word cards onto the matrix if he or she is more kinesthetic/tactile, or conduct an interview with the student explaining the motivations, obstacles, and accomplishments if the student is strong in verbal (rather than written) communication.

Grading Tiered Products

Once a commitment to tiering has been made, the question is "How will I grade all of this?" In order to establish clear procedures on grading, you must first reflect on your overall philosophy. To help summarize some of the perspectives about effectively grading tiered assessments, consider the "If-then" chart on page 120.

Belief Systems on Grading: A Teacher's Self-Assessment

Think about the belief system that you and your team, grade level, department, and/or school embrace. Compare and contrast your beliefs with practices. Based on your responses, determine what changes, if any, need to be made in how you grade.

Do you believe that grades should reflect what students have learned?	If so, then grades would be based on individual student achievement related to the learning goal. Such policies as "extra credit," zeroes for incomplete work, and group grades would be challenged, since they do not relate to the learning goal.
Do you believe that the goal is for students to achieve content mastery?	If so, then there is no time limit on mastery. In other words, students are given multiple attempts to master a concept. Once the student is able to demonstrate mastery, a new grade would likely replace the previous grade.
Do you believe that continuing to receive poor grades can have a negative impact on students?	If so, then consider how you might adjust formative assessments so they are providing more feedback to students along the way and correcting any misunderstandings. Guskey and Bailey (2001) suggest the possibility of a two-part reporting system, so that both a grade and level are assigned to reduce the possible negative impact of a poor grade.
Do you believe that grades should show individual achievement?	If so, then the idea of grading students based on product, process, and progress is related to their personal best. In this way, a learner "profile" may be charted to show individual achievement and growth as well as expected rate.
Do you believe grades should help serve as a communication tool?	If so, then it will be helpful to accompany them with a narrative with additional suggestions of how parents might help at home. In addition, high-quality feedback beyond the grade is the norm.
Do you believe that there are fairer systems for assigning grades (other than averaging)?	If so, then teachers must look for consistency in the evidence they've gathered. If that evidence is consistent across several indicators and a student's scores or marks are fairly uniform, then deciding what grade to assign is a relatively simple task. If the evidence is not consistent, however, then teachers must look deeper and search for the reasons why (Brookhart, 1999). They must also face the difficult challenge of deciding what evidence or combination of evidence represents the truest and most appropriate summary of students' achievement and performance. Recent evidence should be given priority or greater weight, as well as, evidence related to the most essential learning goals or standards. Similarly, comprehensive evidence that has been acquired and built upon over a period of time should be weighted more substantially (Guskey and Bailey, 2001).

What Makes a Quality Tiered Assessment?

Criterion	Exceeds Standards	Meets Standards	In Progress	Does Not Meet Standards
Alignment	Assesses big ideas of the standard in authentic context, with student using vocabulary in applied activity. Scaffolds with above- and below-grade-level standards based on student needs.	Assesses the big ideas of the standard in authentic context through application, with vocabulary from the standard integrated throughout directions and assessment.	Assesses the standard. Vocabulary from the standard is included.	Does not assess all parts of the standard. Vocabulary from the standard is not included or stated in the same way as the standard.
Thinking Skills	Thinking skills are addressed through most appropriate form; assessment extends students' thinking beyond the standard.	Thinking skills are addressed through the most appropriate form of assessment: selected response, constructed response, performance assessment, or personal communication.	Thinking skills are partially addressed, or assessment is not the optimal form for addressing the thinking.	Thinking skills of the standard (implied by the verb) are not integrated in the assessment.
Test Development	Students play a role in the test development process; general guidelines of test development are followed.	Follows general guidelines of test development (as well as those specific to type of assessment). Assessment is concise, with like objectives clustered together.	Mostly follows general guidelines of test development (as well as those specific to type of assessment). Assessment could be streamlined.	Does not follow general guidelines of test development (or those specific to type of assessment). Assessment is disorganized and cumbersome to follow.
Appropriate Learner "Fit"	Provides options for students, when appropriate, that continue to address the thinking skills but also support student strengths. Assessments are tiered to accommodate all learners, including both advanced and struggling.	Provides options for students, when appropriate, that continue to address the thinking skills but also support student strengths.	All students complete the same assessment with accommodations provided, as needed.	All students complete the same assessment in the same way.
Assessment	Self-assessment is incorporated so that students, as well as teacher, have clear understanding of learning and set independent goals.	Use information from assessment to determine students' strengths and needs; understanding is logged and tracked over time; followed by "different" instruction and reassessment.	Use information from assessment to determine students' strengths and needs.	Assessment is used after learning—"summative"; student scores are documented.

A Word About Grading

Since grading is such a huge question I want to direct you to some excellent resources:

Guskey, T., & Bailey, J. (2001). *Developing grading and reporting systems for student learning*. Thousand Oaks, CA: Corwin Press.

Marzano, R., & Haystead, M. (2008). *Making standards useful in the classroom*. Alexandria, VA: Association for Supervision and Curriculum Development.

Tomlinson, C. (2001). *How to differentiate instruction in mixed-ability classrooms*. Alexandria, VA: Association for Supervision and Curriculum Development.

Reeves, D. (Ed). (2007). *Ahead of the curve: The power of assessment to transform teaching and learning*. Bloomington, IN: Solution Tree.

Tomlinson, C., & McTighe, J. (2006). *Integrating differentiated instruction and understanding by design*. Alexandria, VA: Association for Supervision and Curriculum Development.

Wormeli, R. (2006). *Fair isn't always equal: Assessing and grading in the differentiated classroom*. Portland, ME: Stenhouse Publishers.

Summary

"In 'formative'" is how Stiggins (2003) describes the use of our assessments—to both inform us and allow us to adjust our teaching to accommodate learner needs. Quality assessments can answer the questions to support scaffolding and the determination of the next step in learning for a student. A strong assessment is valuable not only to the teacher, but also to the student who can begin to own the learning process. Use the matrix below as a guide to support your reflection about providing tiered assessment for your students.

Ideas for Reflection

1. Review the Framework of Assessment Approaches and Methods on page 101. Think about content that you will be teaching in the next few weeks. How can you adapt the way you assess what students know so that you are using something other than a selected-response format?

2. Decide on a standard or competency that you will be teaching students. While designing the lesson, write down all the expectations you have for student performance. Answer the question: What must they know and be able to do to successfully demonstrate that they know this content? Now create a list of Look Fors for students.

3. Consider a lesson that you have taught or will be teaching. Look at the graphic Matching Assessment with Student Strengths on page 106. Create a menu of products from which students can choose to demonstrate knowledge of content. (Note: Be sure that the choices are equally rigorous and relevant to the content.)

4. Examine the chart What Makes a Quality Tiered Assessment? on page 121. Identify some personal targets for growth as you endeavor to advance your efforts to differentiate.

5. What kind of conversations are you having with your colleagues about assessment for differentiation? How can you expand the discussion?

Chapter 7

Tiered Instruction: How to Get There From Here

Ask any of your colleagues if they think it is important to differentiate instruction in order to meet the needs of individual learners and you will likely get full agreement. If you and your coworkers are committed to holding your feet to the proverbial fire, the obvious follow-up question is this: How does our practice align with our beliefs? I regularly talk to teachers who conceptually embrace the idea that the content they teach ought to be tailored to achievement levels of individual students, but they sigh deeply, saying, "I just can't work any harder!" Perhaps you can identify with their struggle.

Though the effort is challenging, if you have the desire and the intention to move forward in your effort to tier instruction, you can be successful. To make the goal manageable, let the following thoughts serve as your mantras:

- I must start with small successes and increase my efforts; I cannot do it all at once.

- I must work with a partner, critical friend, or learning community; I am not expected to do it alone.

Growing as Differentiators

Be patient. Just as there is tiered instruction for students, we also have to recognize that there are tiers of growth for us as well. Although we want to be working toward particular goals, each of us has his or her own continuum of growth. You need to give yourself permission to be at different places on the continuum. As long as you stay committed to the idea of continuous improvement, you'll improve.

The transition from proficient teacher to highly effective teacher begins with assessing where you are and where you want to go. Similarly to how they use

Learning Continuum: Individual, Team, or School Self-Assessment

	Tier 1: Proficient	Tier 2: Highly Effective
Content	Uses the curriculum guide to identify standards	Unpacks the curriculum guide to identify essential learning outcomes, key language, and vocabulary; finds the big ideas and makes content relevant to learners
	Uses data to examine areas of strength and weakness in the understanding of content	Uses school-wide goals to build on areas of strength and target weaknesses across all grades or teams; uses data as a tool to inform decisions about teaching and learning
Process	Explores best practices	Explores best practices, plans for differentiated instruction, and selects strategies that will scaffold learning for students
	Applies best practices in the classroom	Uses classroom walk-throughs, peer coaching, and/or lesson study to continuously and collaboratively improve on classroom practices
Product	Develops quality assessments	Develops pre-, during-, and post-instruction quality assessments—including formative and summative assessments—with differentiated options for students that are clearly articulated in Look Fors and/or rubrics
	Evaluates student assessments	Examines student assessments on an ongoing basis and develops a group action plan based on varying strengths and needs

scaffolding with students, teachers who desire to grow must discern where they get wobbly and establish those areas as targets for growth. Consider the tools in the earlier chapters as guides and supports as you assess both your own and your students' progress, and design lessons accordingly.

A by-product of your efforts to tier instruction for students is that you begin to identify areas in which you are highly confident and effective. If you have skill and confidence in certain areas with regard to differentiation, ask yourself how you can support others. Perhaps you can be the mentor or critical friend to another colleague. In the same vein, you will also find areas in which you want to become more proficient. Decide where and how you will begin and don't be afraid to ask for help.

As an additional tool, use the matrix in the chart above to guide your thinking about where you and your colleagues are in terms of being proficient or highly effective in working toward the goals of differentiation.

The Power of Collaboration

Even if you are fully committed to differentiating in your classroom using tiered instruction, the task is daunting if you are forging the path on your own. Here is where a partner, colleague, or learning community can be your companion on the journey. Reach out to those around you. Collaborating with others is very helpful in focusing ideas and establishing a vision at the grade, department, or school level. Consider the word *team* as an acronym:

Together

Each

Achieves

More

While this phrase may seem like a cliché, it identifies the power to be found in collaboration. The positives of collaboration are clear because we learn and grow professionally when sharing ideas with others. Additionally, hours spent working interdependently on a task can be much more efficient and ultimately take less time than working solely in isolation. A third positive aspect of working collaboratively with colleagues is that everyone understands the same language and has ownership, resulting in greater sustainability and, most important, increased student learning!

Team Versus Group

Sandra McGrath, a middle school math teacher, is a staunch advocate of teamwork. Here's what she has to say:

> *If teachers truly desire to improve student learning, they must also collaborate. Teaching and learning do not occur in a vacuum, and students are not the only learners. Collaborating affords the opportunity for groups of teachers to use the same lens to discuss student success as a grade level or school.*
>
> *In looking at student achievement in the consumer math standard, each teacher shares the instructional strategies used in their individual classrooms, including strategies that engage students, as well as any impediments to student learning they may have discovered. Such group discussions of content and strategy are powerful. One teacher may hear of a different activity, manipulative, or context in which to teach the material. Another may hear an alternative method of explaining the concept. This same group of teachers can then use their experiences to group and reteach students, tiering instruction to meet the needs of each student.*

Collaborating as a "team" is different from working as a "group" within a school. Think about some of the distinctions in the chart below and consider where your school, grade-level, or department team are currently functioning.

A key to collaboration is to establish times and structures for meetings with the goal of determining specific ways that the group can work together to achieve success for all students. Framing the compelling question that will drive discussion and improvement areas is part of the team's task. As a member of the team, be persistent in your efforts to practice strategies with students and at the next team meeting reflect on what worked and what could have been improved.

Consider your team as action researchers who are constantly trying to enhance instruction for students. In this regard, the topics selected by collaborative partners, teams, or learning communities should be ones that are essential to the success of all students. As you focus on tiered instruction, think about avenues or paths to both improve pedagogy and gain insight into student achievement. With your partner or team, agree on areas of "research" for reflection and growth. Some ideas with related links for additional information are below.

Learning Continuum: Individual, Team, or School Self-Assessment

Differences with regard to . . .	Working as a group	Collaborating as a team
Goals	Each group member works toward individual goals (that may or may not align with those of other group members).	All of the team members work toward common goals focused on continuous improvement.
Contribution	Group members work independently, with each doing his or her own work.	Team members work interdependently, providing a necessary support for each other.
Purpose	Group members are focused on learning for "my" group of students (which will hopefully contribute to success of school).	Team members are focused on learning for the entire grade level, department, or school.
Consistency	There is inconsistency in the performance of group members.	Team members are consistent in implementation of best practices.
Results	Group members typically do not share data, but instead examine data on an individual teacher basis.	Team members examine data collectively to determine student strengths and needs and the best strategies for continuous improvement.
Effectiveness	Group members typically do not share their individual strengths.	Team members build on their collective strengths.
Problem Solving	Group members are not necessarily focused on working to solve problems collectively; this is usually an individual task involving self-reflection.	Team members all bring multiple perspectives and group reflections and ideas in considering topics that they have identified as a team.
Conversation	Group members engage in intermittent dialogue, with a focus on individual task completion.	Team members engage in scheduled discussion and dialogue to help determine the best solutions.

Focus on Tiered Instruction Using the Lenses of . . .

Lesson Study	After a teacher on the team develops a tiered lesson, the collaborative group analyzes it with the team to see what elements of tiered instruction are evident. When the lesson is taught, a collaborative colleague observes and debriefs. The lesson is then brought back to the team for follow-up discussion. (Resource: http://www.tc.edu/lessonstudy/faqs.html)
Peer Coaching	Seek out a partner (in a learning community, at the same grade level, or in the department) and participate in arranged observations followed by reflection. During reflection, questions to discuss include, What worked well? How could I have made the tiered lesson more successful for some or all students?
Response to Intervention	Before considering placement of struggling learners in need of intervention, respond to these questions: Have we effectively tiered instruction in the student's classes? Would differentiation through tiered instruction make a difference in this student's learning? Is the tutoring intervention sufficient? (Resource: http://www.rtinetwork.org/Essential/TieredInstruction)
Action Research and Data Analysis	Consider the ways you should use data to establish a baseline of performance before you try strategies of tiered instruction to see what kind of progress students make. What action research steps should you take to assess whether your efforts are working? (Resource: http://nationalstrategies.standards.dcsf.gov.uk/node/88674)
Creating and Evaluating Assessments	Consider what assessments you can create that measure ongoing learning, tap into a variety of modalities, and focus on assessment for learning. Does your grading system box you into certain kinds of assessments? What changes, if any, can or should be made?
Using Case Studies	As a team, analyze all demographic and performance data of one or two specific students. Discuss how differentiated instruction might be of benefit. As an alternative, consider case studies of hypothetical students to help focus the team's thinking.
Portfolios	Keep a compilation of tiered lessons in a portfolio organized by content area and topic. These lessons could be exemplars for teachers working on differentiation or for other learning communities in the school.
Common Tiered Assessments	Work together in teams to analyze achievement on common assessments, develop strategies to improve levels of achievement, and help each other build on strengths and address weaknesses.
Critical Friends	Establish a formal Critical Friends group to discuss complex issues related to instruction. (Resource: http://depts.washington.edu/ccph/pdf_files/CriticalFriends.pdf)
Classroom "Learning Walks"	Set targets related to tiered instruction and use them as filters during walk-throughs. Discuss walk-through observations with your partner or team. (Resource: http://www.mcrel.org/pdf/teacherprepretention/0125NL_ChangingSchools_58_4.pdf)

Students as Partners

As you commit to adding differentiation through tiered instruction to your repertoire of skills, think about how you are encouraging students to become adept at self-regulating their learning and, in so doing, helping them acquire the skills of metacognition. According to Resnick and Hall (2000), "Today, metacognition and self-regulatory capabilities are widely recognized as a key aspect of what it takes to be a good learner. Moreover, there is little argument that metacognitive strategies are both learnable and teachable" (p. 5).

In Chapters 2 and 6, we discussed ways to involve students in assessing their own progress. Providing opportunities for students to become more responsible for their own learning, as well as becoming contributors to the learning experiences in your classroom, will assist you as you try to support them through differentiation. An ultimate goal is for students to be able to scaffold their own learning and tell you where they need to go next!

For optimal performance, students must be considered partners in the effort to improve both teaching and learning. Believing that all students have innate capacity and that academic ability can be grown is a defining element of professional learning communities (Saphier, 2005, p. 88). In this regard, just as teachers need to work collegially with each other to become more effective at teaching, teachers need to collaborate with students. When you make students part of a classroom learning community, you communicate to them the message that by working hard, thinking together, and problem solving, we can all achieve more. Students need to hear early and often in their school years that achievement is related to effort, not innate ability.

Summary

A single formula for success does not exist when it comes to differentiating through tiered instruction. Rather than a solo performance, it should be considered an ensemble act—you, your colleagues, students, and other stakeholders—performing together. Be bold in your endeavor, courageous in facing the challenges, and confident that you are doing the right thing for the learners in your charge.

Ideas for Reflection

1. Look at the descriptors in the learning continuum graph on page 128. At what points do you think you are proficient? In what areas do you believe that you are highly effective?

2. Look at the chart on page 129. Think about the areas in which you can focus tiered instruction. Are there some tasks that you are involved in already? What instructional-action research activities can you and/or your learning team develop?

3. As you consider the commitment to differentiation at the grade-, department-, and school-level, how can you help advance this effort in your setting?

Student Scaffolding Readiness Scale

Student : _____ Teacher: _____ Grade: _____ Date: _____

Category **Background Knowledge**	**Degree of Readiness**									
	1	**2**	**3**	**4**	**5**	**6**	**7**	**8**	**9**	**10**
• Familiarity with the content	Unfamiliar									Very familiar
• Related background knowledge	Limited or none									Substantial experience
• Vocabulary	Mostly unfamiliar									Strong grasp of essential and related vocabulary
• Reading Level	Two or more years below									Confidently above level
Evidence of Higher-Order Thinking	**1**	**2**	**3**	**4**	**5**	**6**	**7**	**8**	**9**	**10**
• Capacity to handle choice with task	Needs guidance									Performs without direction
• Complexity of thinking	Knowing Understanding Applying									Analyzing Evaluating Creating
• Facility with abstract material	Initially needs concrete, tangible evidence									Works well with abstract examples
Interaction With Content	**1**	**2**	**3**	**4**	**5**	**6**	**7**	**8**	**9**	**10**
• Skill level	Entry									Mastery
• Ability to handle pacing of lesson	Additional time needed									Content can be compacted for acceleration
• Scope of resources used	Needs leveled readers and supplemental materials									Needs access to enrichment resources
• Level of direction needed	Step by step strong support of teacher									Overview with only intermittent checks
Degree of Independence	**1**	**2**	**3**	**4**	**5**	**6**	**7**	**8**	**9**	**10**
• Degree to which modeling is needed	Dependent on teacher									Independent
• Degree to which practice is needed	Needs built-in practice with ongoing feedback									Can move to enrichment quickly
• Degree to which rehearsal is needed	Must teach/assess/reteach									Minimal rehearsal needed

Student Scaffolding Readiness Scale Summary

(Scores of 1, 2, or 3 are areas to be developed and are noted as "D"; scores of 8, 9, and 10 are areas of strength and are noted as "S")

Teacher: _____ Grade: _____ Period: _____ Date: _____ Content: _____

Category																					
Background Knowledge																					
• Familiarity with the content																					
• Related background knowledge																					
• Vocabulary																					
• Reading level																					
Evidence of Higher-Order Thinking																					
• Capacity to handle choice with task																					
• Complexity of thinking																					
• Facility with abstract material																					
Interaction With Content																					
• Skill level																					
• Ability to handle pacing of lesson																					
• Scope of resources used																					
• level of direction needed																					
Degree to which																					
• Modeling is needed																					
• Practice is needed																					
• Rehearsal is needed																					

12 Questions to Prompt Decisions About Tiering by Process

How Will I Engage Students?	Notes
1. What information about my students have I learned from the pre-assessments?	
2. What grouping arrangements are optimal at different stages of the lesson? (When do I use whole-group, small-group, partner, or individual tasks?)	
3. What leveled books and resources do I have to support learning? Do I need to secure additional materials?	
4. What strategies will I use to make connections to what students know already (activate prior knowledge)?	
5. What degree of choice should I offer to students at each tier?	
6. What are entry levels of thinking for students at each tier?	
7. What questions can I pose to scaffold or extend thinking?	
8. How much complexity in a task or assignment can students, pairs, or groups manage?	
9. How quickly or how slowly should tasks advance for each tier of students?	
10. How much independence will specific students, pairs, or groups be able to handle and how much support will I need to provide?	
11. What will be the most effective strategies to use to deliver content?	
12. How will I measure student progress?	

A Practical Guide to Tiering Instruction in the Differentiated Classroom © 2010 by Sarah Armstrong, Scholastic Professional

Lesson Planning Template With Guiding Questions

Standard: The same standard may be used for all learners. This standard is derived from the pacing guide, curriculum guide, or scope and sequence. Do the strengths or needs of learners indicate that this standard may require scaffolding or extending?

What are the big ideas? How do these big ideas connect to the real world?
All students learn best when they are able to make connections and apply meaning. These are not the discrete skills that every student should learn, but are instead the overriding ideas or concepts.

Hook:
What common experiences do I want the entire class to have? How can I engage their attention?

Tiers	Content	Process	Product
	WHAT will I teach?	*HOW will I teach the content?*	*What will I ask students to DO?*
	What information does pre-assessment provide about what students already know or need to learn? What is the prior knowledge about the subject?	What background knowledge will I need to provide?	Is the assessment authentic, including real-life connections and big ideas that are informative of student understanding?
	What is a developmental progression of understandings that students need to have to grasp the standard? What are the prerequisite skills as well as the post-requisite skills that students will need to demonstrate? Where do my students fall on this progression? Each tier should begin where students are and progress forward.	How much independence will be offered? Are students able to perform independently, or will support need to be provided?	Does the assessment scaffold or build on prior knowledge by using specific vocabulary?
		What level of thinking will each tier be asked to engage in initially? What questions might I pose to scaffold or extend thinking, as needed?	What assessment method matches with the verb and the level of thinking implied by the standard?
		What amount of choice will be provided to students?	Does the assessment meet criteria for quality test development, including conciseness and clustering of similar objectives?
	What will be the on-grade-level task? What will struggling learners do? What will advanced learners do?	How many steps or how complex of a task can students handle?	Does it incorporate student choice, and is it tailored to meet the strengths and needs of my students?
	How will the complexity of the content vary by tier, using the progression above?	How quickly or how slowly should the tasks progress, based on the needs of the students?	Does it incorporate self-assessment and feedback?
	Will the vocabulary or reading content vary?	What will be the most effective way of delivering the content?	Does the assessment inform my instruction? In what way(s)?

Closure: How will I have students share as a community of learners?

Math Standard: (Grade 6) Solve multistep consumer application problems.

What are the big ideas? How does this big idea connect to the real world?
How can we be economically savvy, spending and saving money wisely?

Hook: You are a "smart shopper"! As the consumer, your goal is to always find the best deal and save money. What are some ways that you try to save money? (e.g., looking for the best deal at different stores, investing, etc.) Today, each of you will be looking at some scenarios and deciding on the best buys and explaining why. You will write explanations using paragraphs, tables, and/or graphs.

Tiers	Content	Process	Product
Tier 1	Students use the green-level task card from below. Provide students with a budgeting template, structure for writing paragraph conclusions, or table or graphing template, if needed. Basic vocabulary will include *consumer, vendor, conclusion,* and *budget*.	Solve multistep consumer problems on tiered task cards. The problems will include planning a budget.	Present data and conclusions in paragraphs, tables, or graphs.
Tier 2	Students use the red-level task card. Vocabulary will include all of the basic vocabulary plus the words *economy* and *finance*.		
Tier 3	Students use the blue-level task card. Expanded vocabulary will also include the words *stock market*.		

Green-level Task Card	*Red-level Task Card*	*Blue-level Task Card*
Look at the table. You want to buy three shirts. You have found the same style of shirt at two different stores. Where would you want to go to get the best deal? How much money did you save in all?	Look at the table. You want to buy three shirts. You have found the same style of shirt at two different stores. Including a sales tax of 5%, what would be the total cost savings if you were to take advantage of the better deal?	Look at the table. You want to buy three shirts. You have found the same style of shirt at two different stores. You have determined that after a 5% sales tax, your total cost savings would be $3.06. What was the cost per shirt at Shirt Factory?

Green-level table

Vendor	Cost per shirt
Shirt Factory	$8.99
Clothing Closet	$9.49

Red-level table

Vendor	Cost per shirt
Shirt Factory	$8.99
Clothing Closet	$9.49

Blue-level table

Vendor	Cost per shirt
Shirt Factory	???
Clothing Closet	$9.49

Green-level	*Red-level*	*Blue-level*
You have decided to go out for the weekend. Here is a list of activities and their costs. What is a close estimate of the total amount you will spend?	You have decided to go out with your friends for the weekend. Here is a list of activities and their costs. You and your friends will each pay 1/3 of the total cost. What is a close estimate of the total amount you will spend?	You have decided to go out with your friends for the weekend. Here is a list of activities and their costs. You and your friends will each pay 1/3 of the total cost. You cannot spend more than $20 in all. The cost of the movies is fixed, but all other amounts vary. Find at least three different ways you could spend your money, if you spend money for all of these activities.

Green-level activities

Activity	Amount
Movies	$14.75
Popcorn and Drink	$ 8.58
Shopping	$46.28
Dinner	$38.12

Red-level activities

Activity	Amount
Movies	$14.75
Popcorn and Drink	$ 8.58
Shopping	$46.28
Dinner	$38.12

Blue-level activities

Activity	Amount
Movies	$14.75
Popcorn and Drink	???
Shopping	???
Dinner	???

Green-level	*Red-level*	*Blue-level*
Be a smart consumer! Use newspaper ads to plan a budget and show ways that you would save money by purchasing from different vendors. You may spend up to $200. Record the item, price, quantity purchased, and total savings. Draw conclusions about your savings, in a paragraph, table, or graph.	Be a smart consumer! Use newspaper ads to plan a party budget. You will need to decide the number of guests you are inviting to the party and then purchase enough materials. Pay close attention to quantities in each package so that you order just enough. Show a comparison using two competitive vendors. You may spend up to $500. Draw conclusions about your savings, in a paragraph, table, or graph.	Be a smart consumer! Use the newspaper or the Internet to track stock market prices of competitive vendors. Examine the stock prices, if you were to make a purchase a month previously. You may spend up to $1000. Record the stock, selling price, quantity purchased, and total gain or loss. Draw conclusions about your investment, in a paragraph, table, or graph.

Standard:

What are the big ideas? How do these big ideas connect to the real world?

Hook:

Tiers	Content	Process	Product

Closure: